PITFALLS

AND

PIT

STOPS

Navigating Your Retirement Journey

MARK TROYER

PITFALLS AND PIT STOPS
Navigating Your Retirement Journey

Expert
Press

www.ExpertPress.net

Table of Contents

Chapter 11.

Chapter 12.

Dedication

To Luke and Zack: A special thank you for all the adventures we have encountered over the years. The journeys were great…the destinations were amazing . . . but it was the "Pit-Stops" along the trek that made my life so sweet. Although we fell into some pitfalls along the way, we always found our way out. This book and the "Four Pit-Stop Process" would not exist without our time in the wilderness. With every hike I can remember, the best parts always involve you.

In life, and on the trail: slow learners make slow travelers. Never stop learning, growing, and exploring! You are my absolute favorite adventurers . . . in the whole world.

Introduction

Getting to the top is optional.
Getting down is mandatory.

Ed Viesturs, mountaineer

I need to tell you the truth.

The truth is: Retirement changes everything. And never have we ever seen such days as we do right now.

Yes, this is a book about retirement planning. But the truth is, I'm not an ordinary "financial advisor." My team and I operate in a very specific part of finance: We call ourselves retirement *guides*. We build out Retirement Trail Maps. Our planning is untraditional and often unorthodox. If you're looking for confirmation of the same old advice you always get, let me save you some time: Don't read this book.

What we're going through isn't *normal*. Times, they are a-changing. I'm tired of seeing families ruined by financial turmoil brought about by losing money and tax devastation. I grow weary watching everyday Americans struggle in retirement because they followed "good old-fashioned advice" that has simply grown *outdated*. Inept. Or as my dad says, "foolhardy."

I'm not about to sit by and allow this to continue. I need to tell you the truth. Even if I frustrate my friendly competitors.

You need to know the truth. And the truth, as you may have heard, will set you free.

The truth is that never have we ever faced a situation like the one we face today. Our society is woefully unprepared for it. It is so dangerous because few Americans have been educated on how to deal with it.

It will affect every single one of us. America has never seen this before. It is a freight train coming down upon us.

What is it? It isn't political. It isn't the shift to a digital dollar. I'm not *only* talking about tax ramifications.

I'm talking about the retirement of the Boomers. Never have we ever seen *that*.

But Japan has.

Due to a variety of factors—including decades of declining birth rates—nearly *one-third* of Japan's population is over sixty-five.[1] In fact, as far back as 2013, the *New York Times* reported that Japan was selling more adult diapers than baby diapers.[2] Not exactly trivia for the family dinner table, but true nonetheless.

---

1   Charlotte Edmond and Madeleine North, "More Than 1 in 10 People in Japan Are Aged 80 or Over. Here's How Its Ageing Population Is Reshaping the Country," World Economic Forum, September 28, 2023, https://www.weforum.org/agenda/2023/09/elderly-oldest-population-world-japan/.

2   Andrew C. Revkin, "Japan's Diaper Shift and Global Population Trends," Dot Earth Blog, December 24, 2013, https://archive.nytimes.com/dotearth.blogs.nytimes.com/2013/12/23/japans-diaper-shift-and-global-population-trends/.

We're not that far behind.[3]

By 2031, all of the 70 million Baby Boomers will have entered retirement age.[4] More Americans are expected to turn 65 through 2027 than in any time in history.[5] We are now for the first time seeing an entire generation of people living twenty to thirty years past our retirement age. Never have we ever seen this play out before.

In 1934, President Franklin Roosevelt declared that the age to begin Social Security would be sixty-five. Did you know that in 1934, the average life expectancy for Americans was only sixty-two?[6]

That's right. Our government was counting on most of us *dying* before reaching the benefits age. Now here we are living twenty and sometimes even thirty years past the age of retirement. Traditional retirement planning is based mostly on Harry Markowitz's Modern Portfolio Theory, designed in 1952. During the *rotary phone era*. Do you seriously think a retirement plan based upon economic conditions in the 1950s—when retirees rarely lived past their mid-sixties—is the one you want to use? Never have we ever experienced anything like the twenty-first century.

Living longer has its cost.

3   US Census Bureau, "U.S. Older Population Grew from 2010 to 2020 at Fastest Rate since 1880 to 1890," Census.gov, May 25, 2023, https://www.census.gov/library/stories/2023/05/2020-census-united-states-older-population-grew.html.

4   America Counts Staff, "By 2030, All Baby Boomers Will Be Age 65 or Older," United States Census Bureau, December 10, 2019, https://www.census.gov/library/stories/2019/12/by-2030-all-baby-boomers-will-be-age-65-or-older.html

5   Lorie Konish, "As baby boomers hit 'peak 65' this year, what the retirement age should be is up for debate," CNBC, February 8, 2024, https://www.cnbc.com/2024/02/08/baby-boomers-hit-peak-65-in-2024-why-retirement-age-is-in-question.html.

6   "United States: Life Expectancy 1860-2020 | Statista," Statista, June 21, 2022, https://www.statista.com/statistics/1040079/life-expectancy-united-states-all-time/.

Someone has to tell you the truth. Someone has to make sure you protect yourself from the potentially seismic economic changes that are coming. Someone has to show you *The Big Lie* in the financial industry. I don't see anyone else doing it.

But *I'll* do it.

The truth is, no book can solve every problem that will come your way. But I can get you on the right path. A flexible path. How? By giving you a Retirement Trail Map, a map that has the paths laid out for you.

Because I am a retirement *guide*.

The purpose of this book is to help you alleviate your retirement fears and worries with a Retirement Trail Map—one that I believe offers the peace of mind that comes with knowing you'll always have the income you need to live the life you desire.

The secure retirement you've *earned*. The retirement you've dreamed of.

Peril on Mount Everest

A 2008 article from *Scientific American* reached a fascinating conclusion about deaths on Mount Everest.

Everest, as you probably know, is the highest peak on this planet. And every year people attempt to reach it. It can be quite treacherous, naturally, and people die every year trying.

The article found that 85 percent of documented deaths on Mount Everest had one thing in common: They'd *reached the top.* They died on the way *back down.*[7]

You see, folks, I believe that mountain climbing and retirement have a lot in common. We spend our entire working lives hiking up this mountain, following this "grow, grow, grow" strategy of accumulating assets, putting more money into our savings and retirement accounts to *keep* them growing, hoping to one day reach the peak. One day, we'll have more money than we've ever had. We will reach the summit of our own Mount Everest and be able to *retire.*

When we finally reach that peak, we suddenly find ourselves looking at everything from a totally different perspective. Sure, the view is just as breathtaking as we'd imagined, but now we face the daunting task of navigating our way back *down* the mountain to safety.

So ask yourself: "Am I ready? Do I have the right tools?" It's time to get yourself ready for a journey like no other. Let's go!

I have written this to prepare you as best I can. I will use stories to get the points across. Hiking through nature is a lot like hiking through retirement. It's not just about the destination; it's about the *journey.* Far too many fail in retirement by running out of money—not because they didn't *save* enough, but simply because they didn't have the right *plan.* Or had no plan at all.

I want you to take just a moment and ponder this question: "What if you don't actually need *more money* for retirement . . . what if you simply need a better *plan?*"

---

7   Jordan Lite, "Death on Mount Everest: The Perils of the Descent," *Scientific American* Blog Network, December 10, 2008, https://blogs.scientificamerican.com/news-blog/death-on-mount-everest-the-perils-o-2008-12-10/.

Seriously. What would you do differently if you knew that to be the case?

We create Retirement Trail Maps, and every week we show ordinary Americans that they can indeed retire with more safety, and more guaranteed income, without needing to save more money. It's amazing. I hope this book can do the same for you.

This is uncharted territory. Never have you ever created an income plan for retirement. (Before retirement, of course, your income plan was usually just called "a job.") Never have you ever learned about managing taxes in your new post-employment world. Can you trust your own instincts? Can you make it through a storm?

You have no idea how you're going to answer these and lots of other questions over the next twenty or thirty years. You may not even know exactly what questions to *ask*.

The sad reality is that about 90 percent of all financial advisors focus on that "grow, grow, grow" strategy. And it often fails in retirement. That is what we are here to fix. Don't let your retirement fail. Don't die on the way down your mountain by running out of money.

The reality is that—if you're nearing retirement—you've graduated from the "grow, grow, grow" era of saving and investing for the long haul. You now enter the master's level courses: You need to create income and watch out for the tax man *more* than you need to grow your assets. On this journey, you may find that you don't need more money, but you will certainly need a better plan, from a retirement guide.

I've made this journey a thousand times in the last twenty-plus years with clients all across America. Along the way, I've developed my Retirement Trail Maps. I've helped folks just like you successfully navigate from their peak to the safety and peace of mind of a secure, stress-free retirement.

The Power of Pit Stops

Whether descending a mountaintop, taking a cross-country drive, hiking the Appalachian Trail, or creating and implementing a retirement plan, you don't want to try to do it all at once. In fact, when my family and I are hiking or taking a trip, the pit stops sometimes become the highlights of the journey.

In my Retirement Trail Maps, the pit stops play a vital role, each working with and building upon the ones before. In fact, you might say they're the highlights of the journey. We'll go into these in detail later, but the four pit stops of the Retirement Trail Maps are:

1. **Maximize Income: Get a Raise to Retire**

2. **Manage Your Wealth: Reduce the Risk and Optimize the Opportunity**

3. **Minimize Taxes: Retirement Tax Planning**

4. **Multiply Your Legacy**

A Tale of Two Couples

Throughout *Pitfalls and Pit Stops: Navigating Your Retirement Journey*, we'll explore these pit stops in depth, illustrating these concepts with the stories of two couples in a way that's hopefully easily understandable and highly relatable. We'll call one couple Frank and Millie, and the other Joe and Deb. You may *be* one of these couples. As you'll see, that can be a good thing or a bad thing.

Both couples were perched upon the mountain peak at about the same time. They just followed different paths.

I didn't advise Frank and Millie myself; I provide their story as a cautionary tale. It's not good. They followed traditional advice and conventional wisdom—like "buy and hold" and "the market always comes back." They weren't crazy with their money: They averaged a 6 percent annual return while withdrawing only 5 percent. Yet in just over a sixteen-year period, they lost it all. I know, that seems mathematically impossible. It's not. I'll tell you why.

Joe and Deb were one of the original Retirement Trail Map couples. My advice was considered somewhat unorthodox, my plan unconventional, but they followed the plan and are still going strong. They should never have to worry about money again: their income is guaranteed,[8] and their investments should continue to grow. I'm going to show you how they did it.

I love what I do. My team and I come to work every day with big smiles on our faces. Why? Because we get to help folks just like you create a simple yet effective plan to protect what's coming in, grow what you have, limit tax liability, and leave a legacy for your family and favorite charities.

Don't try to hike down that mountain alone. Let the Retirement Trail Map be your guide.

---

8 Guaranteed income is offered by an insurance company and backed by the claims-paying ability of that company.

Part I.

Frank and Millie: A "Traditional" Retirement Plan Is No Plan at All

Chapter 1.

Meet Frank and Millie

Imagine that on your way to work you find a bank envelope full of cash. You pick it up, thinking of all the heist movies you've seen. You hustle to your office desk to quickly count the cash. It's $100. All in $5 bills.

Not wanting to be caught by the cops for this illustrious haul, you decide to spend $5 at a time at your local coffee shop.

Let me ask: How many times can you pull $5 out of that envelope?

If you guessed twenty times, you are correct and have earned ten bonus points. Way to go. Nothing could change the math here: You can pull a $5 bill out twenty times.

But that is *not* how retirement works. The math is more complex.

Frank and Millie retired with $1 million. They wanted to withdraw $50,000 per year. If they had stuck all $1 million in an (extremely oversized) envelope or buried it in their back yard, Frank and Millie could have pulled out $50,000 per year for twenty years. The math is the exact same as our envelope above.

But . . . Frank and Millie followed traditional retirement planning. They averaged a 6 percent rate of return over seventeen years, taking out 5 percent ($50,000) annually, and ran completely out of money.

How can this be?

That is the question you should be asking. This isn't just Frank and Millie's story. It's a story that can happen to many unsuspecting Americans every day. And I can't let it happen to you.

Folks, retirement changes everything. Never have we ever faced times like this. We need to be aware of the pitfalls that happen in retirement and avoid them like the plague.

I first met Frank and Millie in 1999, when I was an intern for a successful financial advisor in Indiana. Frank and Millie were both sixty-two years old and had just retired with $1 million in Frank's individual retirement account (IRA). They were at the peak of their financial mountain.

The couple had just started taking their Social Security and were drawing a combined $40,000 per year.

Their goals were simple: They wanted that million-dollar IRA to pay them $50,000 per year (5 percent) and *never run out of money.* I bet many of you want a similar plan: Spend the interest; don't worry about the rest. Frank and Millie wanted to live off that interest ($50,000 per year) and their Social Security.

In hindsight, they *literally* would have been better off burying that $1 million in their garden and pulling out $50,000 each year. Instead of lasting twenty years, it was gone in just over sixteen.

"How can that be?" you ask. You may be thinking that their advisor should have had better math skills.

I need to tell you the truth. And the truth is, math can be deceptive and tricky.

A long-accepted financial standard is called "The Rule of 4 Percent." It states that you should be able to safely withdraw 4 percent a year from the cash value of your investments and never run out of money. My boss at the time told Frank and Millie all about the rule; he also told them he thought he could probably find them an extra 1–2 percent return on their investment above the 4 percent they'd need. In the end, Frank and Millie did *better* than the advisor hoped. They proceeded to *average 6 percent returns over a nearly seventeen-year period*. And they had only wanted to draw out 5 percent.

Now you're probably *really* puzzled. The math says Frank and Millie should have been able to live even more comfortably than they'd planned. After all, they earned even *more* interest.

Math can also be mean sometimes.

Frank and Millie needed help—not from a "grow, grow, grow" advisor, but from a seasoned retirement guide. A guide who knows ways to help avoid the pitfalls of retirement, so you can enjoy the pit stops, the scenery, the fun stuff. Someone who can help you live the retirement you've always dreamed of. Frank and Millie came to one of my educational workshops at the end of 2015. By this point, so much damage was done that they were nearly broke! They asked me to do what I could to make sure this doesn't happen to other people. What I *can* do is show *you* how to avoid the same fate.

In this first section of the book, I'm going to talk about the missteps that were taken in Frank and Millie's case. We're going to discuss the pitfalls in retirement, including what I call the *Triple Crown of Financial Failure*—three things that you can get away with when you're *climbing* the mountain, but which can be deadly to a secure retirement. Then I'm going to show you ways to help enjoy the pit stops leading to the retirement you've always dreamed of.

I'm going to show you—in a way that doesn't require either a calculator *or* a bottle of aspirin—just how tricky and deceptive the math can be. I'm going to explain how distinctions like *Average* versus *Actual* and *Fixed* versus *Variable* are extremely important, and how risk can be the horrible gift that keeps on giving.

I'm going to tell you all about the ONE FACTOR that can turn math on its head and flush your retirement dreams down the toilet.

We all want our golden years to be truly golden. We want them to be safe and secure. We want the peace of mind of knowing that our finances are working *for* us and that—no matter what obstacles we face—our money isn't going anywhere.

We're laying the foundation of a Retirement Trail Map.

And we're going to start by looking at where Frank and Millie went wrong . . .

Chapter 2.

The Triple Crown of Financial Failure: Losses, Fees, and No Guarantees

It's January 21. The year is 2007. Millions of NFL football fans—including myself and a good portion of my home state of Indiana—are watching the AFC (American Football Conference) Championship game: Peyton Manning and the Indianapolis Colts hosting Tom Brady and the New England Patriots. The winner is heading to the Super Bowl.

For the Patriots, a win would be a case of "been there, done that." Since 2000, they'd been the AFC *and* Super Bowl champs *three times*. And the Manning-led Colts? Well, the last time they'd won an AFC Championship (let alone a Super Bowl), there'd been a "Baltimore" in front of "Colts" and their quarterback was a guy named Johnny Unitas.

So yeah, it had been a while.

By halftime, Colts fans were experiencing their own "been there, done that." Thanks in large part to an end zone fumble recovery and a pick six (an interception resulting in a touchdown) by the Patriots, my beloved Colts were down by fifteen points.

Based on history, it seemed like pretty much an insurmountable lead.

It wasn't. Not this time.

Peyton Manning, in a career-defining second half that would cement his place as one of the great heroes of Indiana sports, brought the Colts back from almost certain defeat. By the end of the third quarter, the game was tied. Then, with just a minute remaining in the game, Indianapolis took a 38–34 lead.

Tom Brady had been in this spot before, so we Colts fans weren't high fiving each other quite yet.

Then he threw an interception.

GO COLTS!! (Sorry . . . I still get excited thinking about that game.)

What do you think Peyton Manning did when he went back out on the field with just forty-four seconds left? Did he go for the end zone? Maybe surprise the Patriots with a long bomb or look for a weakness in their secondary with a short pass underneath?

Of course not. Peyton Manning and Coach Tony Dungy were *way* too smart for that.

Manning took a knee. The clock ran out. Indianapolis was on its way to the Super Bowl. (They won that too—*Go Colts!!*)

You know what that AFC Championship game reminds me of?

That's right, retirement planning. (As you might be able to tell, I find retirement analogies in *lots* of things—I'm kind of a geek like that.)

The first half of that legendary football game reminded me of those pre-retirement years, when we can afford to take some risks. When a run of bad luck (like a falling stock market or a pick six) doesn't necessarily spell doom. When we still have time to recover.

The second half of that game reminds me of those years spent climbing our personal Mount Everest, overcoming adversity until the peak is almost within our grasp.

The last minute of that game reminds me of actually *reaching* the peak—finally—and having the presence of mind to take a knee. Because you know that any unnecessary risks could knock you right off that mountain. You know that you're in the "red zone"—the period from five years before retirement to five years after. And you know that when you're at or very near the top of the mountain, *any* risk is unnecessary.

What does all this talk of a great win have to do with Frank and Millie? Well, I'm going to show you how losses, fees, and no guarantees led to a pick six *late* in their game (rather than in the first quarter).

I'm going to show you how unnecessary risk-taking helped snatch defeat from the jaws of an almost certain victory.

Losses

As I mentioned earlier, Frank and Millie retired in 1999 at age sixty-two with $1 million (not counting their combined $40,000 in Social Security). Like many retirees at the time, they were advised to do a "rollover" (basically a tax-deferred transfer) of the million dollars from Frank's IRA into a *variable annuity*. "Variable" means the annuity's value is tied to the fluctuations of the market. Their plan was to take $50,000 per year (5 percent) from the growth of this annuity.

Now, this seemed a sure bet in 1999. From 1950 to 2000 (what I like to call the "rotary phone years") the S&P 500 had done nothing but grow, grow, grow. In fact, $1,000 put into the market in 1950 would have grown to *over $83,000* in 1999.[9] So sure—there was *some* risk; it just didn't *seem* risky. Frank and Millie felt secure that they'd be able to live out their retirement *without even TOUCHING the principal*.

The year 1999 itself wasn't bad. Frank and Millie started the game with a couple of completed passes and a first down. The market gained 8.1 percent.

From 2000 through 2002, the S&P fumbled the ball. It tumbled over 40 percent in just those three years.[10] With their $50,000 yearly payout, plus the fees (which we'll talk about soon), Frank and Millie fell dangerously behind. Their $1 million was effectively cut in half.

But they were still in it. Still on the mountain.

---

9 "S&P 500 Total Returns by Year since 1926," Slickcharts.com, n.d., https://www.slickcharts.com/sp500/returns.

10 "S&P 500 Total Returns by Year since 1926," Slickcharts.com, n.d., https://www.slickcharts.com/sp500/returns.

Their financial advisor tried to paint a rosy picture (as advisors often do): "It'll come back," he told them. "*It always comes back.*"

Imagine you're Frank and Millie, getting a statement showing that your $1 million investment is now only worth $473,000.

What do you *do?* If you sell, you're cutting your losses. Admitting defeat. When you're younger, you have the opportunity (and plenty of *time*) to earn this money back. But remember: *Retirement changes everything.* You're not earning—you're just trying to survive on the money that *your money* earns. You feel desperate but see no way out except to gamble. To throw a Hail Mary. To just hang in there.

And that's what Frank and Millie did. From 2003 through 2007, it looked like there was a chance the gamble might pay off: The market rallied *over 60 percent* during those five years.[11]

But the comeback was short-lived. It was also deceptive. For one thing, the 60 percent they gained wasn't on their original million-dollar investment; it was on the roughly *half a million* they had left after three straight years of losses.

In 2008, the S&P threw a pick six. The market lost nearly 40 percent *in one single year.* And—even though the market rebounded by over 100 percent from 2009 through 2015—it still knocked Frank and Millie off the mountain.[12]

Read that again: **The market rebounded by over 100 percent, and it *still* knocked Frank and Millie off the mountain!**

---

11 "S&P 500 Index - 90 Year Historical Chart," Slickcharts.com, n.d., https://www.macrotrends.net/2324/sp-500-historical-chart-data

12 "S&P 500 Total Returns by Year since 1926," Slickcharts.com, n.d., https://www.slickcharts.com/sp500/returns.

By 2015, even with an average return of 5.9 percent, even with a market which had shown net losses for only four out of the fifteen previous years, Frank and Millie's $1 million investment was only worth $135,000. Had they buried that money in their garden and taken out $50,000 each year, they'd have been better off.

Coming up shortly, we'll dive deeper into why the numbers aren't always what they seem. We'll look closely at something called a *sequence of returns* and learn how timing can be everything. Later on, you'll see why—with a Retirement Trail Map covering the four pit stops—*timing doesn't need to be a factor AT ALL*.

But now, let's have a look at the second "jewel" (or lump of coal) in our *Triple Crown of Financial Failure*.

Fees

Fees are tricky little devils. They seem so innocent. They seem so *reasonable*. After all, what's 3 percent (a typical fee for some popular retirement products, especially in the early 2000s)? It's less than half of *sales tax*!

But fees are the "high blood pressure" of retirement planning: While they may *seem* harmless (and are often hidden), they can be silent killers.

Beware of fees.

Just have a look at the following chart, which shows the return on two nearly identical investments of $250,000 from 1990 to 2020. The first has a 3 percent fee. The second offers no fee. Over the span of three decades, this account with a 3 percent fee would have grown nicely: In fact, it would have nearly *quadrupled*, up to just over a million dollars.[13]

But look at the same investment on the S&P 500 with *no fees*.[14]

Figure 1. S&P 500 Returns 1990–2020

Wow!

That same $250,000 investment would have grown by *a factor of TEN*! $2.6 million!

Maybe you're thinking, "Wait a minute. Three percent of $250,000 is less than $9,000. How in the world can that small amount make such a HUGE difference?"

Remember what we talked about earlier in the chapter: Your money simply doesn't grow as fast if there's *less of it to grow*. This

13 "S&P 500 Total Returns by Year since 1926," Slickcharts.com, n.d., https://www.slickcharts.com/sp500/returns.

14 It is not possible to invest directly into the S&P 500. This is for hypothetical educational purposes only.

is one of many small reasons why we say, "You don't need more money; you need a better plan."

When you think about it, **fees are just another form of loss**. A Retirement Trail Map can minimize (or possibly even *eliminate*) both. Overall, fees are only ever a problem in the absence of value. For example, if someone could double my money every year, I wouldn't mind paying that person 10 percent in fees. There must be value if a fee is being charged.

You might be wondering, "Who would ever pay a 3 percent fee?" It's more common than you would think. Even today this is happening inside of unsuspecting retirement accounts. I recommend asking if your account has things like mortality and expense fees, guaranteed living withdrawal benefit fees, subaccount fees, death benefit riders, etc. The list of fees you could be paying is long. And let's just say it isn't "front page of the statement" material.

Right now your brain should be sounding the alarm. Make sure you are not paying for those things unless they are absolutely necessary for your retirement plan to succeed. It rarely works out in your benefit.

If you are not sure if you're paying these fees, you owe it to yourself to find out. Or you owe it to the company you are invested with. The choice is yours. We often say to people, "You don't need more money, you just need a better plan." I'll add to that line: "a better plan without unnecessary fees!" How awful it would be to get 15 years down the road and realize, "I had enough money, but I paid too much in fees. Now I'm off course."

No Guarantees

There's a famous quote, often attributed to Ben Franklin (but that Google tells me was coined earlier by an English dramatist named Christopher Bullock), which states that "in this world nothing can be said to be certain, except death and taxes."

What Ben and Chris meant, of course, is that there are no guarantees. Apart from death and taxes.

This just isn't true.

For instance: If Frank and Millie had chosen to bury their million dollars in their garden, they would have been *guaranteed* $50,000 per year for twenty years. That's just math. Instead, they ran out of money in just sixteen years.

There are, in fact, annuities sold by insurance companies that will *guarantee* to pay you back with a lifetime stream of income no matter what happens.[15] Or they'll *guarantee* that you can change your mind and get all your money back (minus, of course, fees).

Frank and Millie's financial advisor could have steered them toward a plan which would have *guaranteed* them $40,000 annually, for life. Instead, he sold them on a variable annuity that had the *potential* to give them the full $50,000 each year that they wanted. Like I said, it wasn't a *huge* gamble—the market had been going strong, with occasional dips, for decades.

But it *was* a gamble. And Frank and Millie lost. So ask yourself . . . is that a gamble you are willing to take with your hard-earned life savings? What if there is a better plan?

Part of the Retirement Trail Map I'm going to detail for you in the next section of this book offers **no losses and no fees**. It takes

---

15 These guarantees are backed only by the claims-paying ability of the insurance company.

almost all of the traditional retirement risks *entirely off the table*, giving you the peace of mind that comes with knowing that—no matter what happens—you're going to have a steady stream of income you can rely on.

Chapter 3.

The Big Lie and the Big Secret: Average Returns Aren't Actually "Actual"

I grew up in the tiny town of Topeka, Indiana. (The population then was about a thousand.) For me, there were only a few fun things to do: attend the Fourth of July events, watch lightning storms, catch lightning bugs, play some basketball, and cheer on my best friend Andy Begley. Andy was a state champion cross-country runner, and I loved to watch as he raced—and nearly always beat—the horses and buggies that still made up a large portion of the traffic on our community's roads.

I, on the other hand, am not much of a runner. A few years ago my sister and I made a pact. We wanted to get into better shape. Being highly competitive, we made a deal: We were going to start running and hold each other accountable. Over the course of the year, we planned to average ten miles each per week. Now, ten miles per week wasn't going to make me a champion runner like Andy, but hey, we all have to start somewhere.

We each got a logbook. We started doing our thing. At the end of the year, sis and I agreed to sit down and go over how we'd done.

My sister was so excited! I told her, "Sis, you look great, you've obviously been killing it. Go ahead, tell me what your logbook says. How many miles did you run this year?"

With a giant grin (of just the sort a sibling might have when she's been waiting for a year to beat her brother in a competition), she said, "Mark, I did it! Not only did I run ten miles per week . . . I got so into it, I ran *twenty* miles per week!"

"Holy smokes, sis! I am so excited for you. You definitely beat me!" I replied.

Then the moment of truth came. And like I said, I have to tell you the truth.

"So . . . come on, I've waited all year," she said. "How did *you* do? How many miles?"

"Sis, I have great news!" I told her with a big smirk on my face. "We did it! We *both* hit our goal! We averaged ten miles per week!"

She looked at me, raising an eyebrow questioningly.

I clarified: "Because you ran twenty miles every week, and I didn't run *at all*, we *averaged* ten miles each." I showed her my own blank logbook.

"I couldn't have done it without you, sis!"

As loving sisters often do, she punched me in the arm and called me a dork.

You see, being completely honest and being *truthful* are not always the same thing. When you take sis's twenty miles per week, add in my zero miles, then divide it by two, it's true that our combined average was twenty miles per week. But it wouldn't be completely *honest* to say that my sister and I averaged running ten miles every week.

You've heard it said that numbers never lie. But they certainly do *deceive*. You've probably known someone like this—they don't lie, but they don't tell the *truth* either. They deceive. Deception is a terrible trait in a person. But it can be absolutely *devastating* in retirement.

What I'm about to show you may get me in trouble with my peers. But hey, it's time we all know what's going on. I'm going to show you both *The Big Lie* and *The Big Secret* that work against any and every retiree . . . that no brokers or advisors are telling you about. Why don't they? I can't answer that. Maybe they don't have solutions. Maybe they don't understand the journey.

Financial brokers have been using this technically-true-but-misleading reasoning for decades to sell investors on the stock market being a sure bet.

"Honesty" and "truth" aren't *always* the same thing. But I promise you, "average" and "actual" almost *never* are. When it comes to your retirement, "average" is a dirty (and dangerous) word.

The Big Lie

By law, statements from brokerage firms must show you your one-year, three-year, five-year, and lifetime *averages*. (Go look at your statement; it says "average.") As you can see below, they use simple math. What happens if the market sees a 100 percent gain on an investment of $100,000 (it never does, but this is just for our example), then loses 50 percent the next year (that part's a little closer to reality)?

$100,000 x 100 percent return = $200,000

$200,000 x -50 percent return = $100,000

Before doing any more math, can we just use normal common sense for a second? Forget taxes. Forget fees. If you start with $100,000 and end with $100,000, did you make any money?

NOPE! I think we can all agree that our *actual* return was zero dollars. Zero percent. But guess what? That's not what Wall Street says. Your brokerage statements do the math differently. Every 401(k) statement you've ever looked at will tell you your math is wrong. BY LAW, they must report your *average return.*

To get the *average* rate of return (ROR), we would add 100 percent, subtract 50 percent, then divide that by the two years we were invested.

100 percent - 50 percent = 50 percent

50 percent / 2 years = 25 percent

According to our average ROR, we've made 25 percent each of those two years. Congratulations! Yet we know *we didn't make a dime.* Thank you, Wall Street, for misleading us all these years.

HOW CAN THIS BE?! Worse, how can the lie be this brazen and no one knows it? After all, it's fifth grade math. THIS,

DEAR READERS, IS THE BIG LIE OF THE FINANCIAL WORLD.

Seriously, in over twenty years, I have never been through a training program—nor known a training program any of my peers have been through—that explains this as simply as I've just explained it to you.

Could it be that the "higher ups" don't *want* you to know?

Average returns are not actual! This is *The Big Lie* of the financial industry. They don't want you to know what is happening to your money!

Wall Street and the local neighborhood brokers want you to think you are *averaging* a good return. Wall Street and your local advisor will tell you, "Yep, it's a fact: Mark and his sister averaged running ten miles per week."

So what do we do? We must find the problem! And it is so simple, you're going to have a hard time believing you didn't think of it.

The Big Secret

Ever kept a secret before? Ever had to keep a secret where maybe your brother was deceiving your parents? Remember those days? Welcome to the financial advisors' secret club.

Here's what happens: We understand that averages aren't actual. We know. We all know. None of us should get a pass for not knowing . . . It's simple math. But what do we do? Does the financial industry tell you about it? Do they also tell you the solution?

Nope. They tell you to "buy and hold." "Hang in there for the long haul." They require you to "wait it out, the market always comes back up." And my favorite, "Oh, it's only a paper loss."

Folks, the people who say those lines are probably really good people. Those lines can indeed work while you are saving in the "grow, grow, grow" phase . . . but it's ludicrous advice for a retiree. And if you're still hearing those lines you need to run! You need to find a retirement guide.

Are you ready for me to reveal the "Big Secret"? Here it is:

It's all about the losing.

If you *ever* lose money, your average return will *not* be your actual return. Let me say that differently: If you *never* lose money your average and actual returns *are the exact same*. Average returns and actual returns are often so far apart it's the difference between lightning and lightning bugs. The difference between prosperity and poverty. We just saw how you could average a 25 percent ROR but have an *actual* return of zero. What if you paid fees for that "privilege"? Worse, what if you were taking income? YIKES!

It doesn't matter how much you make; it's what you *keep* that counts. If you made money in 2021 and then lost it all in 2022, did that do you any good? Nope! The markets were up nearly 28 percent in 2021 and lost about 18 percent in 2022.[16]

The simple average here is 10 percent over two years, or 5 percent average ROR. Not enough, but not terrible. But the reality for most people is this:

$100,000 + 28 percent (-1.5 percent fee) = $126,500

$126,500 - 18 percent (-1.5 percent fee) = $101,832

---

16 "S&P 500 Total Returns by Year since 1926," Slickcharts.com, n.d., https://www.slickcharts.com/sp500/returns.

$1,832 total return over two years: That's LESS THAN 1 PERCENT PER YEAR *actual* return. Not the 5 percent average return they tell us. All while inflation was well north of 5 percent. This is devastating to most retirees' plans. It's like a thief in the night . . . you don't even know what just happened. The numbers look fine, but the reality is very different. Lightning vs. lightning bugs.

In retirement it's all about the dollars, never the percentage.

As we discussed in the last chapter, losses—whether in the form of the market or fees—play a MAJOR role in your retirement plan. The bigger the loss, the worse it gets—and the further apart "average" and "actual" become.

Retirement requires a new set of tools. It's no longer about "grow, grow, grow." It's about *limiting your drawdown*. It's about *protecting yourself* from the huge drops in the market which seem to be occurring more and more frequently.

What kind of losses are your investments subject to?

Remember: Frank and Millie started with $1 million and *averaged* a 6.1 percent return over a nearly seventeen-year period. They only withdrew 5 percent of their initial balance, or $50,000 per year. The math *seemed* to be on their side. After all, for most of those years they made a positive return. A traditional retirement plan would say this is pretty good. A Wall Street broker would offer them a hearty, "Congratulations!"

Frank and Millie would beg to differ. In about seventeen years, they were broke.

It wasn't just the *timing* of the losses (although, as we'll see in the next chapter, that was a *huge* factor).

It wasn't just the fees (although, as we saw in the last chapter, that played a big role too).

It wasn't just the lack of guarantees for their investment (although that was a culprit as well).

It was the *size* of their losses. The more you lose, the worse it's going to be.

If you never lose money, your average and actual are the same!

Is your advisor telling you that? Is that person showing you the tools you need in retirement that have 100 percent principal protection, so you never lose money? (For a deep dive into accounts that won't lose money and earn a reasonable return, see chapter 8. I've been recommending these for over twenty years. They can work as part of *your* portfolio.)

A Retirement Trail Map doesn't use smoke and mirrors to make things appear what they're not. It doesn't try to manipulate the numbers in a way that isn't completely *honest*. Retirement planning is all about small details across many different areas that make the enormous difference between success and failure—between enjoyment and devastation.

When it comes to your retirement, "average" just isn't going to cut it.

Chapter 4.

Back in Time: How Sequence of Returns Can Be Your Retirement's Real Villain

O kay. I've admitted that I'm a geek when it comes to finding retirement planning analogies in the seemingly strangest of places. But I'm also a movie geek.

Let me demonstrate.

One of my all-time favorite movies is *Back to the Future*. I know you've seen it at least once. If you're anything like me, you've seen it more times than you can count. You have much of the dialogue memorized. You can't read or even *hear* the words "back in time" without immediately playing the chorus of Huey Lewis and the News' hit song from the movie in your head.

If you're anything like me, you're hearing it now.

My new friend Pete (an attorney referred to me by a client) is a big fan of that movie, too. The very first time we chatted, our conversation quickly went from sports—the Colts of course—to *Back to the Future*. We each quoted a few of our favorite lines. (It's rare that I get to tell a prospective client, "Manure. I hate manure.")

I knew I was going to like this guy.

Then we got down to business.

"You know, Mark," Pete said. "I've been doing *really* well with my investments."

He went on to explain that he had most of his money tied up in the Nasdaq (where you'll find most of the high-tech companies). Over the last half a decade or so he'd been getting close to a 20 percent return each year.

"With those kinds of returns," Pete continued, "I don't have to limit myself to just withdrawing 4 percent a year. Heck, I can take out *5 or 6 percent*, and my money will keep growing."

He looked at me solemnly. "There doesn't really seem to be much risk there. Why wouldn't I just continue doing what I'm doing?"

"Well, you *could*," I answered honestly. "But you're not taking into account the sequence of returns."

I could tell by his blank expression he had no idea what I was talking about.

"Huh?" he said.

"The markets have a tendency to go up and down in groups of years," I told him. "That can come back to bite you. Big time."

Pete rebutted with a familiar argument: "But Dave Ramsey says that over time, I can *still* expect to earn 10–12 percent."

I knew he was *really* hoping I'd agree.

"Dave Ramsey's not *wrong*, is he?" Pete asked.

I normally wouldn't talk to a client or prospect like this, but I felt that Pete and I had bonded and that I could get away with it. I did my best Biff Tannen impression.

"*Hello?*" I said. "Anybody home?"

Pete smiled, so I continued.

"Think, McFly, *think*." Then I added another line from the movie: "Don't be so gullible."

I had Pete's full attention now.

"It's time, Pete," I told him. "Let's take a ride in my DeLorean. We're going back in time!"

Then, as I knew would happen, we simultaneously broke out in song, belting out "The Power of Love" in our best Huey Lewis voices.

"Let's start with an easy one," I said. "Remember the Great Depression?"

"Well, I wasn't *alive* at the time, but of course."

"What if I told you that if you'd had money in the market back then, it would have taken you *twenty-five years* of investing just to get back to *even?*"

"Wow." He looked stunned. "Really?"

"And that's *if* you'd been able to see the future and make all the right calls." I continued with one of my favorite Yogi Berra quotes: "It's tough to make predictions, especially about the future."

"Well, yeah . . ." Pete stammered. "But that was the *Great Depression.* We learned from that, right?"

"Did we, Pete? Let's go back to more recent history, say 1965. Pretend you had invested in a blue-chip stock fund. Something that had similar returns to the Dow Jones Industrial Average." (The Dow Jones features thirty "blue-chip" or solid companies from many different market categories.)

"The Dow Jones was right around 1000 that year. The next seventeen years, between 1965 and 1982, were basically the high-water mark. It significantly dropped a few times—especially in the mid-seventies—but always rebounded to 1000, which is where it was in 1981.[17] Your investment could potentially have had very similar results."

---

17   "S&P 500 Total Returns by Year since 1926," Slickcharts.com, n.d., https://www.slickcharts.com/sp500/returns.

Figure 2. The Dow 1965–1982

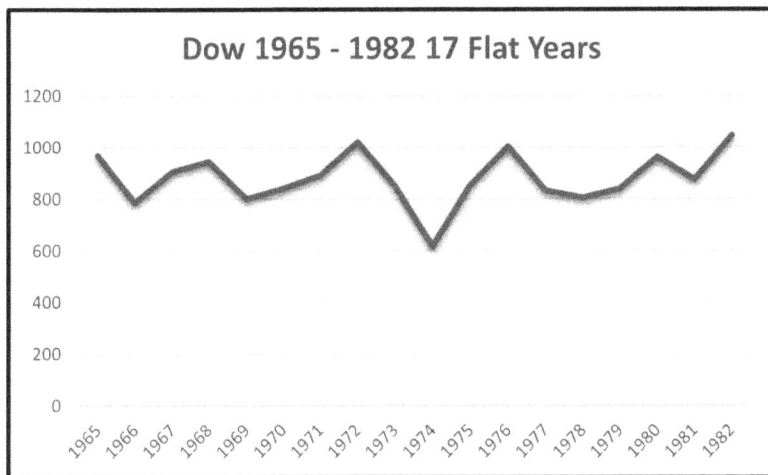

Dow 1965 - 1982 17 Flat Years

"The Dow would not stay above the 1000 level until 1982, seventeen years after first reaching that high level. If you had a similar large-cap growth fund that followed the US market, your performance would be similar. Can you imagine waiting seventeen years to make any new money . . . now that you are retiring? Yikes!"[18]

"Okay, Mark, I see what you're saying," Pete said, nodding. "There are cycles of growth and loss, right?"

"You got it, Pete," I answered. "The fancy word for it is 'non-linear.'"

I broke out one of my analogies:

"The stock market is like a great spy or superhero movie with an excellent twist. Two best friends get along for ages. That's you and the market. Then there's a falling out—maybe it's a girl,

---

18   Past performance is not indicative of future results. The chart shows the Dow Jones from January 1, 1965, to December 31, 1982. It is not currently possible to invest directly into the Dow Jones Index.

maybe your best friend goes over to the dark side. Anyway, the bottom drops out. You're no longer friends. Now you're enemies."

I explained to him how, in retirement, your lifelong friend could turn on you. And how time will no longer be on your side.

I could see he was beginning to get it.

"This scenario has been playing out over the entire history of the market," I went on. "What goes up is usually going to come down. Then it takes you longer to recover, because you're simply left with *less money to grow*."

"Wow." Pete was stunned.

"Pete, what would've happened if you'd retired in 1965 with the plan of only spending your gains?"

He shrugged, so I answered.

"You would have gone *sixteen years without any gains to spend!* You know what that means?"

He nodded, sadly. "I probably would've been dead."

"Exactly."

Now it was Pete's turn to do an impression.

"Great SCOTT, Marty!" His Doc Brown voice was remarkably spot-on. "I'm sixty-eight years old and I've been in the game a long time—why wasn't I warned about this?"

"Well, first of all," I answered, "Most financial professionals don't even *realize* what kind of damage such losses can do over time. And the ones that *do* are so used to repeating the conventional wisdom of 'Buy and hold,' or 'You're in it for the *looong* haul,' or 'Don't sell now, it's only a paper loss,' that it's almost like they're on autopilot."

I went on, "If your advisor is still stuck on 'grow, grow, grow' as you near retirement age, then he may have outlived his usefulness as an advisor."

Pete frowned.

"I'm not saying he's a bad *person*, Pete," I said. "I'm just saying he really doesn't *know* how to help you with this type of situation. It's just not what the average advisor is geared for—keeping your investments *safe* and 'grow, grow, grow' are kind of mutually exclusive."

"Hmm," he replied, still obviously troubled.

"And there's another reason he might not know about this," I continued. "It's really a kind of *new* problem. We're just now reaching the point where the vast majority of seniors aren't retiring with a *pension*.[19] Historically, the stock market was for people who had money to play with. It didn't affect most seniors."

"That makes sense," Pete said, nodding again.

"And according to a recent headline in *The Wall Street Journal*, 'A Generation of Americans Is Entering Old Age the Least Prepared in Decades.'[20] No doubt this is because of a lack of pensions—those guaranteed paychecks from your employer after you quit working. To that point, a recent study found that "only 4 percent of private workers now rely entirely on a defined-benefit plan for retirement."[21]

19 Jeanne Sahadi, "Traditional Pension Plans Are Pretty Rare. But Here's Who Still Has Them and How They Work," *CNN Business*, September 7, 2023, https://www.cnn.com/2023/09/07/success/pensions-retirement-savings-explained/index.html.

20 Heather Giles, Anne Tergesen, and Leslie Scism, "A Generation of Americans Is Entering Old Age the Least Prepared in Decades," *Wall Street Journal*, June 22, 2018, https://www.wsj.com/articles/a-generation-of-americans-is-entering-old-age-the-least-prepared-in-decades-1529676033.

21 Steven Malanga, "The Retirement Crisis that Wasn't," *City Journal*, January 10, 2024, https://www.city-journal.org/article/the-retirement-crisis-that-wasnt.

I could see that Pete was starting to get it. I also had a feeling that it hadn't *completely* sunk in. That happens a lot.

So I told him about Frank and Millie.

"Let me show you, Pete, just how *much* of a villain this 'sequence of returns' can be."[22]

Figure 3. Sequence of Returns Risk[23]

| | Real Returns | | $ 1,000,000 | Inverse Returns | |
	Annual Return	Year End Value	Withdraw Income	Annual Return	Year End Value
1999	8.1%	$ 1,001,100	$ (50,000)	1.3%	$ 933,100
2000	-9.1%	$ 829,867	$ (50,000)	13.8%	$ 983,968
2001	-12.0%	$ 655,553	$ (50,000)	32.4%	$ 1,223,550
2002	-22.3%	$ 439,895	$ (50,000)	15.9%	$ 1,331,143
2003	28.7%	$ 503,035	$ (50,000)	2.1%	$ 1,268,764
2004	10.8%	$ 492,373	$ (50,000)	14.9%	$ 1,369,366
2005	4.8%	$ 451,186	$ (50,000)	27.1%	$ 1,649,520
2006	15.7%	$ 458,667	$ (50,000)	-37.2%	$ 936,083
2007	5.5%	$ 419,951	$ (50,000)	5.5%	$ 909,111
2008	-37.2%	$ 201,046	$ (50,000)	15.7%	$ 974,931
2009	27.1%	$ 199,519	$ (50,000)	4.8%	$ 942,383
2010	14.9%	$ 173,202	$ (50,000)	10.8%	$ 966,077
2011	2.1%	$ 121,591	$ (50,000)	28.7%	$ 1,164,552
2012	15.9%	$ 87,252	$ (50,000)	-22.3%	$ 820,270
2013	32.4%	$ 62,930	$ (50,000)	-12.0%	$ 647,393
2014	13.8%	$ 19,733	$ (50,000)	-9.1%	$ 518,994
2015	1.3%	$ (30,601)	$ (50,000)	8.1%	$ 495,514
	5.91%	Average Rate of Return:		5.91%	

I explained what he was looking at.

---

22 The following is a hypothetical example provided for illustrative purposes only; it does not represent a real-life scenario and should not be construed as advice designed to meet the particular needs of an individual's situation.

23 "S&P 500 Index - 90 Year Historical Chart," Macrotrends.net, n.d., https://www.macrotrends.net/2324/sp-500-historical-chart-data. Data is based loosely upon the returns of the S&P 500 over those years and should be considered hypothetical in nature.

"On the left, you see a summarized version of what happened to Frank and Millie. They started retirement with a million-dollar nest egg. They withdrew $50,000 per year with an average ROR of just below 6 percent. They paid some fees. Twelve of those sixteen years the market *gained*, but they were never able to recover from those early losses. By then end of 2015, they'd lost almost all of it."

"That's heartbreaking," Pete said somberly.

"It was," I said. "But look at the column on the right. I kept all the variables the same, I just flipped the market returns upside-down—into a different 'sequence.' And when you start to withdraw money, like we all do in retirement, it absolutely changes everything we know about the markets. Both columns *average* the same return of nearly 6 percent. But retirement changes everything, and *when* you take money out matters more than the *return*. How do we ever know when the markets will go down? We don't! It's like trying to predict when lightning will strike!"

Pete was dumbfounded. "Unbelievable."

"Yep," I answered. "Unbelievable to the tune of over *half a million dollars!*"

"Well, that's great information, Mark," he said. "I'm sure glad I'm not in the Dow Jones or S&P! I just don't think the Nasdaq is anywhere *near* that risky—they've been on fire for years!"

"I thought you might say that, Pete," I said, pulling out my Nasdaq chart. "Have a look at this."

Figure 4. Nasdaq Investing Risk[24]

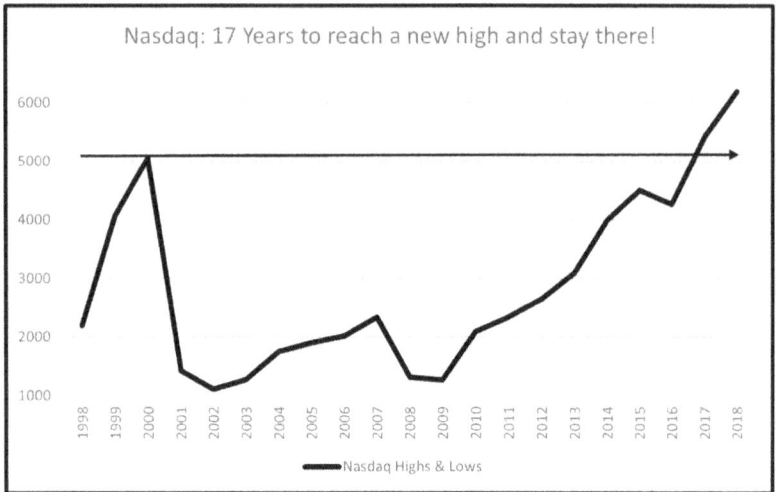

Nasdaq: 17 Years to reach a new high and stay there!

■■Nasdaq Highs & Lows

I explained.

"Pete, if you had invested in the Nasdaq in 1999, you'd have seen it peak the following year. But *then* look at what it did."

I could tell he hadn't seen this chart before.

"After that," I told him, "You'd have gone more than *sixteen years* without any income from that investment! The Nasdaq hit a peak in March of 2000, and by October 2002 had dropped over 75 percent."[25]

"Ouch," he said.

24 Past performance of the Nasdaq index from January 1, 1998, to December 31, 2018 and may not be used to predict future results. It is not possible to invest in the index itself.

25 Tara Clarke, "The Dot-Com Crash of 2000–2002," *Money Morning*, June 12, 2015, https://moneymorning.com/2015/06/12/the-dot-com-crash-of-2000-2002/.

"Ouch is right. Now, in 2000, you'd have been a fairly young man, still in your late forties. You probably could've weathered that kind of storm."

Pete nodded again. "Yep."

"But Pete." I paused to let the seriousness sink in. "What if that happened now? Would you be able to weather *that* storm? Would you have the time?"

He sighed and shook his head. "I'd probably be dead," he said.

"Neither one of us wants that, my friend."

Pete seemed to make up his mind. "So what do we *do*, Mark? I'm probably going to retire next year. How can I protect myself if this happens again?"

"Best question you've asked all day, Pete!" I answered. Then I told him about my Retirement Trail Map. "It's designed to help you weather any storm the market brings and help you safely navigate through the retirement you've always dreamed of."

I wasn't able to help Frank and Millie, but I'm happy to say that I helped Pete feel secure with his retirement. He's still a good friend and never fails to thank me for introducing him to the Retirement Trail Map.

True to our *Back to the Future* roots, we end every meeting not with a standard "Goodbye" or "See ya" but with a hearty "Why don't you make like a tree and get outta here?"

And of course, we often call each other "Butthead."

Chapter 5.

Farewell to Frank and Millie

As much as I'd like to close out this section on the relatively lighter note of the last chapter, I just can't. I'd be doing a disservice not only to Frank and Millie, but to *you*. For Frank and Millie's tale is a cautionary tragedy. Sadly, there was no happy ending.

Frank passed away in 2019, at age eighty-two, the final chapter of his life riddled with fear and uncertainty. Their retirement savings was almost gone. What had started out just twenty years prior as a nest egg of a million bucks had—through a combination of bad luck and traditional advice—dwindled away to almost nothing.

Their golden years were anything but golden. They'd been at the peak of their mountain and come down the hard way.

They'd both taken Social Security at age sixty-two. That was a misstep. After Frank's passing, Millie received the larger of the two monthly Social Security checks, but—after Medicare—that was only $1,800. Because of her failing health and her lack of a long-term care plan (another misstep), Millie now lives with her daughter.

On paper, it had seemed like a *good* plan. After all, a million bucks growing at a minimum of 5 percent should have easily allowed them to live on $50,000 per year. That would have left virtually the entire principal to cover all those "what ifs" (like long-term care) we don't like to think about. There should have been plenty left over for the kids and grandkids when they were both gone.

There'll be no inheritance now. It's all Millie can do to buy Christmas gifts.

Millie wanted me to tell you that if you want to know what *regret* looks like, just look at her.

Even with the missteps mentioned above, Frank and Millie could have had a happy retirement. They could have weathered the impact of taking their Social Security early, they could have been able to afford long-term care when it became necessary. They could have left a legacy.

They didn't need more money. They needed a better plan.

(What about you? Do you need more money? Or just a better plan?)

Their biggest mistake—and the one that compounded all the others like a wicked snowball rolling downhill—was *where* they put their money. Had they been protected against market losses and fees, against the vicious impact of that sequence of returns, they could have made it.

But they weren't. And they didn't.

Had they retired in 2010 (instead of 1999), they *also* could have survived. The market has done pretty well since then—it hasn't suffered the downturns that plagued Frank and Millie's retirement from the outset.

And yet the *risk* would still have been there. And the uncertainty with it.

Frank and Millie's story is the reason I go to work each day. My life's mission is to help retirees *avoid* these risks.

The Retirement Trail Map does exactly that. It takes the sequence of returns off the mountain. It anticipates the unexpected. It answers those retirement questions that begin with "What if?" It eliminates the missteps.

In the next section, I'll explain—through the story of Joe and Deb, a couple who reached the top of their mountain at about the same time as Frank and Millie—how you can have the security and peace of mind that comes with keeping your money safe while it grows and provides you with an income you can't outlive.

Traditional retirement planning has—for as long as there have been retirement planners and advisors—advocated the investment strategy of "buy and hold." It's made a lot of folks (both investors and brokers) a lot of money. But that strategy ignores risk. It ignores sequences of returns. It ignores many of those "what ifs" that can obliterate peace of mind in the blink of an eye and topple your retirement off the mountain.

I offer my clients this warning instead: "Buy and hold, go broke when you're old." That may *seem* rather cute and pithy, but it's deadly serious advice.

Just ask Millie.

Part II.

Never Have We Ever: A Modern-Day Retirement Plan

Chapter 6.

Meet Joe and Deb

Not everyone stands atop their personal Mount Everest with a million bucks. And sometimes—as Frank and Millie's sad story shows us—even a million isn't enough.

When Joe and Deb came into my office in 2000, they had $500,000 saved. They were both sixty-two and ready to retire. Neither of them had a pension, and they were worried that $500,000 might not get them through. They were worried that the next two to three decades—what were supposed to be their golden years—would be filled with never-ending anxiety, as they wondered if they would run out of money before they ran out of life.

They had every reason to be worried.

Of course, no one could have known then that 2000 would wind up being one of the worst years to retire in well over a quarter century. No one could have known about all the couples who (like Frank and Millie) would fall victim to a declining stock market, crippling fees, and a vicious sequence of returns.

Despite many a broker's and financial planner's assertions to the contrary, *nobody* has a crystal ball.

Joe and Deb didn't need to look into the future to know that they wanted something different. They wanted to make sure they never ran out of money, even if they got sick and needed long-term care. They wanted to avoid unnecessarily risking their nest egg. They wanted to pay a minimum in taxes. And they wanted to build a legacy and leave money to their kids and church.

Joe and Deb just wanted to be *happy*. They just wanted peace of mind.

I take great pleasure in telling you that happiness and peace of mind is exactly what Joe and Deb found.

This didn't happen by mistake. It wasn't an accident. It wasn't that fortune smiled down upon them, even as it seemed to curse Frank and Millie.

Rather, it was a *plan*. A modern-day retirement plan.

A Retirement Trail Map.

As you'll see, even though Joe and Deb had half the savings of Frank and Millie, they decided upon a far superior plan. They didn't need more money. They needed a better plan.

I trust you'll find hope for yourself in the following pages.

Defying Traditional Retirement

Tradition can be a wonderful thing. It can be Christmases with the family, opening gifts and singing carols around the tree. It can be the handing down of precious heirlooms from generation to generation.

Over the last half of the twentieth century, there was much to be said for traditional retirement planning as well. Common adages like "buy and hold" and "stay the course" became traditions because they *worked*. Advisors and planners told their clients "The market beats everything over time" because it did.

Until it didn't.

If you're in your forties or older, you probably remember rotary phones. They were a longtime tradition. And they did the job.

Until they didn't.

The rotary dials were replaced by keypads. Then cell phones started replacing landlines. By the '00s, cell phones had become virtually indispensable for much of the population. Today, there are fewer landlines (and even fewer rotary phones) than ever before.

Far too many retirement plans—like Frank and Millie's—base their strategy on tradition, on economic principles like Modern Portfolio Theory (which we'll discuss in more detail later) and on outdated investments like mutual funds. These traditions, theories, and investments rose to popularity and thrived during the rotary phone era.

Times have changed. Retirement planning should change, too. For never have we ever faced the challenges—and opportunities—of the twenty-first century.

Modern-day retirement planning does have similarities to traditional planning. But the *differences* are the game-changers.

The new millennium we're in has seen unprecedented (at least for our lifetimes) challenges and opportunities, gains and setbacks. The past few years have been unprecedented on steroids.

The *next* few years will likely be unprecedented as well.

Most economists agree that taxes must go up. There is no other realistic option given the *quantitative easing* (in layperson's terms, the printing of money) since the Great Recession, combined with years of record-low interest rates, combined with the unprecedented spending in the aftermath of the COVID-19 pandemic. And who will bear the brunt of those higher taxes? Despite some politicians' promises to the contrary, we all know that it *won't* be the big corporations. More likely, it's going to be the middle to upper middle class. It's going to include a *lot* of folks who are approaching the peak of their personal Everests and ready to retire.

Most likely, it's going to include *you*.

According to a US Census Bureau report from 2020, adults aged sixty-five and older will outnumber children for the first time in American history by the year 2034.[26]

What else is unprecedented? Never have we ever seen so many retire without a company pension, and never have we ever seen so many expected to live so long *after* retirement.

And never have we ever seen so many so financially unprepared for it.

Joe and Deb didn't know this. Again, they just knew they wanted to try something *different*. Descending safely down your

---

26 Jonathan Vespa, Lauren Medina, and David M. Armstrong, "Demographic Turning Points for the United States: Population Projections for 2020 to 2060," Census. gov, February 2020, https://www.census.gov/content/dam/Census/library/publications/2020/demo/p25-1144.pdf.

personal Mount Everest isn't a sled ride—it's one cautious step after another.

It's making pit stops along the way.

And that's how we helped Joe and Deb safely down the mountain.

In this section of the book, I'm going to show you how it was done. I'm going to explain how what I call the four key pit stops of a modern-day retirement—*Income*, *Investments*, *Taxes*, and *Legacy*—combined forces to give Joe and Deb the happiness and peace of mind they'd always dreamed of. One cautious step at a time.

If this sounds like *your* dream retirement, I welcome you to join us for the journey.

Chapter 7.

Retirement Pit Stop #1: Income

The Phoenix Suns, begun as an NBA expansion team in 1968, don't have a lot of trophies to show for their fifty-plus years in the league. Sure, they've been to the playoffs thirty times, but they've only made it to the NBA Finals three times and have never won a championship.

Yet in the 2004–2005 season the Suns forever changed the way the game of professional basketball is played.

And they did it in *seven seconds or less*.

Prior to that season, professional basketball could be rather predictable (while still obviously exciting enough to attract millions of fans). Offenses moved slowly down the court, passing the ball multiple times as they tried to set up shots, the action punctuated by brief fever-pitched moments of shooting and defending.

In 2004, newly promoted head coach Mike D'Antoni had a different vision. With the help of free agent Steve Nash (acquired from the Dallas Mavericks), along with Shawn Marion and Amar'e Stoudemire, the Suns instituted an offensive strategy that D'Antoni dubbed—you guessed it—*seven seconds or less*.

The whole goal of this strategy was to keep opponents' defenses in a perpetually scrambled state by shooting *fast*. The Suns would force the defense to quickly react to a fast-moving offense.

And it worked. In their first full season under D'Antoni, the Suns played at the league's fastest pace (by a wide margin), hit more three-point shots than any other team had ever hit in a season, and won thirty-three more games than the year before. At the time, this was the third-biggest turnaround in NBA history. D'Antoni was named Coach of the Year and Nash won the first of his two consecutive MVP awards.

But guess what happened? Suddenly, the rest of the NBA followed suit. They picked up their paces, too. By 2020, *seven seconds or less* just didn't cut it. In the words of an article written by Joe Wolfond in *The Score*, "The game has sped up to the point that the 2004–05 Suns would have been the slowest team in the league in 2019–20. To watch the NBA today is to watch the ongoing ripple effects of that seismic moment in league history."[27]

You can't watch an NBA game today—with offenses operating at breakneck speed, getting down the court quicker, and taking more shots than would have once seemed possible—without

27 Joe Wolfond, "Almost Famous: 7 Seconds or Less Suns Came Up Short, But Changed the NBA," *The Score*, n.d., www.thescore.com/nba/news/1969570.

giving a tip of the hat to the Phoenix Suns and the revolutionary vision of Mike D'Antoni.

I'll bet you're wondering what in the world this has to do with Joe and Deb and the Retirement Trail Map. Well, I'll tell you.

For nearly as long as the NBA (which started in 1946) has existed, the financial world has been doing things pretty much the same way. We've been in a *pre-seven seconds or less* phase, you might say.

It all started in 1952 with Harry Markowitz's Modern Portfolio Theory (MPT), which won him a Nobel Prize in Economics. In lay terms, MPT states that it's better to diversify your portfolio over a wide range of investments; the gains of the best investments will overcome the losses of the underperformers.

This has been the model for investment strategy ever since. And—for a *long* time—it worked pretty darned well.[28]

But guess what? The financial world (along with most everything else) has changed immensely since 1952—especially in the last twenty years or so. The very foundation on which MPT was based, that the market will *always* correct itself over time, has experienced a seismic shift. The market *doesn't* always correct itself. It rarely corrects itself *enough*—in a short enough period of time—to make up for the damages incurred by more-frequent stumbles. Losses, fees, no guarantees, taking income . . . these all stop MPT from working as predicted.

The old way of doing things ruined the retirement dreams of Frank and Millie (and countless others) during the waning years of the last century and the first two decades of this one. The innovations of the Retirement Trail Map—and its new perspectives

---

28 Rebecca.Baldridge, "Understanding Modern Portfolio Theory," Forbes Advisor, June 26, 2023, https://www.forbes.com/advisor/investing/modern-portfolio-theory/.

on the old way of doing things—led to Joe and Deb's winning season.

And it all starts with our first pit stop: the #1 secret to a happy and successful retirement.

The Key Components of a Successful Retirement

Over the twenty-plus years of my career, I've consulted with thousands of retirees or soon-to-be retirees. I've discovered the secret sauce to a successful retirement.

I'd love to say that the secret is something really clever that no one else has figured out. But I'd be lying. In fact, the #1 secret to a happy and successful retirement is simple; it's something your grandma would've told you at the kitchen table.

Are you ready for the secret?

The #1 secret to a happy and successful retirement is to have more guaranteed income than your expenses.

Pretty simple, huh? Now, I'm not saying you need more income than you have *now*. I'm saying you need more income than *expenses*. And it has to be *guaranteed*.

Can you imagine going to work for two weeks and not getting a paycheck? When you ask your boss about it, he says, "Well, we didn't have enough money coming in, so I can't pay you."

Then he adds, "We hope to have enough coming in soon."

Many people live like that in retirement: hoping the income will come in. That's why *guarantees* matter. Over the years, some of my most joyful and happy clients seem to have been those retired from the police force or fire department. They have great pensions. They know that no matter what happens this month, they have enough money coming in to pay their bills. They don't have the stress of having to pull money out of the market when the markets are down. They don't have to worry about *timing* anything.

Folks, I repeat: the number one thing you can do to set yourself up for a good, long retirement is to make sure you have more guaranteed income than expenses.

That should be the first thing that you do; it's the first thing we do with all of our clients. But if you don't have a pension, how do you *get* this guaranteed income?

A few ways: First, we optimize Social Security, possibly with a "hybrid retirement" that includes working part time during your early retirement years. Second, we minimize your taxes (not something you want to try at home). Finally, we get you a *personal pension* to "fill the gap" between what you're bringing in and what you *need* to bring in.

Let's begin with Social Security.

Optimizing Your Social Security

I told you at the beginning of this section that Joe and Deb's retirement goals were fairly simple: First and foremost, they wanted to never run out of money while avoiding any unnecessary risk to their nest egg. That's not surprising—most studies show that running out of money before running out of life is *the #1 fear* of retiring Americans. Obviously, optimizing your income is the best way to remedy that fear.

Actually, unless you're sitting on millions of dollars, it's the *only* way.

Joe and Deb were most definitely *not* sitting on millions of dollars.

The first step to maximizing your income lies in optimizing your Social Security. Please note: I didn't say *maximizing* your Social Security. Sure, if everyone waited until they were seventy to start receiving their monthly check from Uncle Sam, they would all be getting bigger checks than if they'd started earlier. But the *size* of the payment is only a small part of the equation. Sometimes it's a more effective strategy—based upon your total retirement picture—to add a smaller amount of income earlier.

Filing for Social Security Benefits: Let Me Count the Ways . . .

I'm sure you know that there's more than one way to file for Social Security. But how many ways *are* there?

Go ahead. Take a guess.

You might think there are tens or even dozens of ways. I mean, it's the *government*, after all. What would any government program be without a bunch of forms?

You might think there are as many as a hundred different ways to file. Again, it's the government.

But what would you say if I told you *there are 567 ways* for a married couple to file for Social Security benefits?[29] Shocking, huh?

---

29   Tim Kulhanek, "Be Proactive When Planning How to Claim Social Security Benefits," Kiplinger.com, May 4, 2020, https://www.kiplinger.com/article/retirement/t051-c032-s014-planning-how-to-claim-social-security-benefits.html.

A Lifelong Investment

My best estimate is that the average working American couple has deposited nearly $750,000 into the Social Security system.[30] Three-quarters of a million dollars! Filing for your benefits is a HUGE decision!

With so much invested and so many ways to file, where do you turn to get advice on the *best* way to recoup your investment?

Why, the Social Security Administration, of course!

Just kidding. Don't do that.

The Social Security Administration (SSA) will gladly collect your taxes, and they'll gladly start sending you checks once you're eligible. What they *won't* do—what they *can't* do—is lend a helping hand with the paperwork.

The SSA has a handbook called the *Program Operation Manual System* (POMS).[31] This little volume clearly defines what the administration's employees can *and cannot* do for claimants (that's you).

The section on customer service states that it's the SSA employee's job to "provide enough information so that claimants can make informed decisions." Then it says, "but **do not give advice**." (I'm adding the emphasis there, although there's every chance the rep you're on the phone with has a sheet of paper with "DO NOT GIVE ADVICE" thumbtacked to the wall of their cubicle.) One of the first things we do while creating your Retirement Trail Map is a *Social Security Optimization*

---

30 Assuming a two-person household, averaging $60,000 annual income over a forty-one year work history contributing 15.3 percent to Social Security via their FICA taxes and employer-paid FICA taxes.

31 "Social Security Online Services," Social Security Administration, n.d., https://secure.ssa.gov/apps10/poms.nsf/Home.

Report. Within just a few minutes—with information provided by Joe and Deb—I was able to narrow down their options for filing Social Security to just a few. Much better than the 567 they started with.

At that time (this was in 2000), we decided that their most effective option was for Deb to begin taking her Social Security right away (they were both sixty-two), with Joe delaying taking his for a few years. The reason I say "at that time" is because— believe it or not—the rules have changed since then. The best strategy in 2000 most likely won't be the best strategy if you're retiring today. Or a few years from now.

This strategy allowed Joe and Deb to have some Social Security income right away (Joe was eligible for spousal benefits in addition to what Deb would receive) and even more a few years down the road.

And how would they bridge that gap until Joe started taking *his* benefits?

I'm glad you asked.

Do the (Side) Hustle

No, I'm not talking about that dance craze from the seventies. "Side hustle" is just a way of saying "side job," but with a little more pizzazz.

Joe and Deb had already retired from their career jobs, but Joe still wanted to do *something*. He was still healthy; he still had plenty of energy. He just knew he didn't want to work full time for his lifelong employer anymore.

Every year, there are more and more Americans who feel the same way. And I can tell you that having a "side hustle" is absolutely one of the *best* ways to bridge the income gap between full-time work and full retirement. It creates income; it adds to your Social Security; it can offer huge tax benefits. Mostly, it enhances the *certainty* of your retirement plan.

(Some of you are thinking, "This doesn't resonate with me at all." Don't worry. You don't have to do the side hustle if you hate the idea. Stick with me until the end of this chapter.)

Joe was very fortunate. When he announced to his employer that he was going to retire in a month, they asked him if he would consider staying on as a consultant. Turns out his boss valued what he brought to the table. So after Joe talked with his CPA (which I recommend you do as well), he became self--employed as a consultant.

He still got to see some of the same faces. He still got to do the same type of work to which he'd devoted forty years of his life. But now he was his own boss. As his own boss, he was able to benefit from tax breaks allowed for his home office, laptop, equipment, and even some lunches. He could even deduct part of two vacations that he and Deb took (he squeezed in a few hours of consulting during the trips).

Even more personally rewarding for Joe was that he bought his dream vehicle—a Ford F250—and was able to write off the cost because he also needed it for his job. (We'll talk more about taxes later.)

Joe did this hybrid retirement until age seventy. In the meantime, he optimized his own Social Security check. He and Deb lived on his income while Deb spent her Social Security check spoiling the grandkids and enjoying life.

For all our readers: This extra side hustle increases earnings, which increases the final Social Security payments, which also enhances savings, and adds to the wellness of your retirement plan. It increases . . . everything. Except, perhaps, the most important thing: your time. Hybrid retirement will take up more of your remaining hours with work than plain old retirement. You will continue to have some of the job responsibilities and commitments you've been managing for decades. Only you can decide if it's worth the tradeoff: less free time now, in return for a healthier income number now—and hopefully much more free time later. Many people decide it's worth the trade.

Now, this isn't for everybody. Some folks, after a lifetime of working, just don't want to *work* anymore. At all. That's absolutely fine and understandable. The Retirement Trail Map isn't a one-size-fits-all plan. It's custom-made. But *everyone* journeying along this Retirement Trail Map will still enjoy the secret of retirement contained in pit stop #1: **The #1 secret to a successful and happy retirement is to have more guaranteed income than expenses.**

If your monthly expenses are $5,000, well, you'd better know *for sure* that you've got more than $5,000 coming in each and every month. That's how you rest easy. That's how you stay secure.

This isn't one man's opinion; it's backed up with math and science by the foremost thinkers and economists in the world of finance, who nearly all agree that the absolute best way to retire is to have more guaranteed income than expenses. Guys like Moshe Milevski, Dr. Wade Pfau, Dr. Lawrence Kotlikoff, Nobel Prize in Economics winner Robert C. Merton, and a host of others agree. (More on this later.) So let's get with the changing times. Just like the Phoenix Suns changed the game, it's time we change our retirement plan.

Obviously, Social Security optimization and side hustles are just part of the equation. The third step of our Maximize Income pit stop has to do with making your nest egg earn its keep—creating lifelong income without jeopardizing the money that's *earning* you money.

If you want to do the side hustle, great. It can increase your odds. However, what we have found is that nearly 85 percent of the people who come to see us *thinking* they need to keep working, don't. You don't need more money; you simply need a better plan, from a retirement guide, who can get you the guarantees you need NOW.

Like the Phoenix Suns and the *seven seconds or less* strategy, it's about making the defense adapt to *you*, rather than the other way around.

It's about creating your *personal pension*.

And that's what we're going to talk about next.

Chapter 8.

Your Personal Pension: The Muscle Car of Retirement

The first pit stop is all about the importance of having a *guaranteed* income in retirement. We saw that the first two steps to guaranteed income are optimizing your Social Security, plus perhaps supplementing that income with a side hustle. The third step on this crucial first pit stop of your Retirement Trail Map is so cool and important that it deserves its own chapter.

Few things in life are for sure. "Death and taxes" make the cut. But I'd like to add one more. I would call it a "sure bet," except that it's not a "bet" at all. It's a contractual promise. To be specific, it's a special type of insurance policy—one that can provide you with an income for the rest of your life.

I call it a personal pension.

* * *

In the early 1960s, Carroll Shelby was already a household name for his success as a race car driver. He'd been the *Sports Illustrated* Driver of the Year in both 1956 and 1957, set multiple national speed records at the Bonneville Salt Flats, and won a slew of international road races, including the "crown jewel" in 1959: the 24 Hours of Le Mans.

In his travels across Europe, Shelby toured numerous limited--production automotive plants. He concluded that "America was missing a big bet, a winning bet: the design and production of an all-purpose, all-American sports or grand touring car that you could drive to market and also race during the weekend."[32]

The designers at Ford took notice. They had plenty of great vehicles made for the average American, but none with the *high performance* they knew a large segment of the population was craving. So they recruited Shelby. His idea was to put a 300-horse--power engine on a lighter, Austin-Healey type chassis. The result was a high-performance car that weighed in at less than 2,600 pounds. (By contrast, a Ford Thunderbird at the time weighed nearly 4,000 pounds.)

Shelby's collaboration with Ford resulted in the Shelby GT350 (in 1965) and the Shelby GT500 (in 1967), both iterations of the Mustang Cobra series. The American muscle car was born.

I know you're saying to yourself, "So, Mark . . . what does any of this have to do with *retirement?*"

I'm glad you asked.

32 Carroll Shelby, *The Carroll Shelby Story* (Los Angeles: Graymalkin Media, 2020).

In 1996, a man named Richard Kado was one of the original architects of the first *fixed indexed annuity* (FIA).[33] As Shelby's Cobras changed the landscape of automobile manufacturing in America, so too did the FIA change retirement income planning.

Annuities have been around since the days of the Roman Empire but have gotten a bad rep from some critics over the last couple of decades.[34] Some of this criticism is justified. I mentioned in chapter 2 how Frank and Millie's *variable* annuity helped lead to their fall from the mountain. To this day, I'm not a fan of 99 percent of all annuities.

But the FIA is an entirely different beast. And a few—just a few—FIAs are what I call the muscle cars of retirement.

They're like a personal pension.

What did Mr. Kado do that was so different and innovative? He approached solid A+ rated insurance companies—the insurance industry's equivalents of Ford in the auto industry. He basically told them, "You have annuities that are nice for many average Americans. But they don't have the *performance* that many other Americans need." That had been the problem with annuities for decades—they lacked the performance that made driving (owning) them fun.

Mr. Kado set out to fix that. The annuities he designed certainly added the required performance. For centuries, insurance companies have insured your life and your most valued possessions. But most of those policies didn't earn any type of *interest* —not until Mr. Kado and his Genesis Financial Development

33   Jim Maschek, "Annuity Awareness Month: The FIA Turns 25 This Year," The Quantum Group, June 16, 2020, https://thequantum.com/annuity-awareness-month-the-fia-turns-25-this-year/

34   "A Brief History of Annuities," Due, March 24, 2022, https://due.com/annuity/a-brief-history-of-annuities/.

group stepped in and raised the bar (filing more than fifteen patents for annuity products along the way).

For most of their existence in America, annuities paid a set rate of return—just like a bank account or CD. The problem with *that* was that the rate wasn't enough to keep up with inflation. With Mr. Kado's FIAs, owners have the same guarantee that they won't lose principal—but now they can also earn *interest*, based upon the movements of a given financial market "index" (most commonly the S&P 500).

You may never have heard of Mr. Kado, nor his patents, nor his work. Why? Because the FIAs that contain Mr. Kado's patents are still very elite. Just like the Shelby Cobra GT500 of 1967, they are a rare bird indeed. But well worth it (both the FIA *and* the vintage muscle car).

Since the advent of MPT (which we covered a bit in the last chapter), the common wisdom has been to divide your investment portfolio 80/20 (with 80 percent in the stock market and 20 percent in bonds) during your *accumulation* years, gradually transitioning to 60/40 (stocks/bonds) the closer you get to retirement.

But as we also mentioned in the last chapter, times have changed.

The truth is, the last couple of decades of poor bond performance have shown us that bonds are a *terrible* place for income-producing assets. What we need is a bond *replacement*.

Like a personal pension. A personal pension that has the *performance* to keep up with your income. Isn't that what most of us want? Something reliable, that lets us spend the interest and maintain our principal? If so, keep reading!

For many retirees (including Joe and Deb), a personal pension is a major component of their Retirement Trail Map, ensuring that they won't run out of money before they run out of life.

If you want to find the very best investment options for your life savings, you need to find yourself an independent fiduciary who can act as your retirement guide.

Let's get into some of the details. I'll also tell you about the two catches.

The same way I told my friend Pete.

For Pete's Sake

Remember Pete, my sixty-eight-year-old attorney friend with whom I'd bonded so well over our mutual love of *Back to the Future*?

Shortly after our initial meeting, we met up a second time and discussed these remarkable FIAs and the role they play in the Retirement Trail Map.

"Okay, Mark," he said. "You've told me about the importance of creating a safe and reliable stream of income for my retirement years. You said there's an investment that *totally* has this covered." He arched his eyebrows. "So what is it?"

"Pete, what do you know about annuities?"

He made a face, kind of like I'd spiked his coffee with lemon juice. I've seen that face before. I *expected* him to make that face.

"Well," he grimaced. "I know that I've heard some bad things about them." He shrugged. "But on the other hand, my uncle had an annuity that paid him a regular income every month until the day he died. At ninety-seven."

I smiled and nodded.

"Most of what I've heard is bad, though," he continued. "People say they're terrible investments."

"Well, first of all, Pete," I replied, "they're not investments *at all*."

"Huh?"

"They're *insurance*."

Pete looked surprised.

"But guess what?" I added. "I hate most annuities myself."

Pete looked surprised again. I continued: "About 70 percent of all annuities are *variable* annuities. Their value is directly tied to the stock market."

"That's bad, right?"

I chuckled and nodded. "In *retirement*? It's the worst. I wouldn't touch a traditional high-fee variable annuity with a ten-foot pole."

"Got it. Variable annuities bad."

"*Very* bad. You remember the story I told you about Frank and Millie?"

Pete nodded again. "Absolutely."

"They had *their* retirement savings tied up in a variable annuity. Not only were they hit by that vicious 'sequence of returns' we talked about, but they were also paying over 3 percent in fees."

"And fees are bad."

"Yes, Pete. Fees are bad."

"So what about the other 30 percent?" Pete asked.

"About half of those—or 15 percent—are 'fixed' annuities. Now, they're *okay,* I guess. At least I don't *hate* them. The problem with those, though, is that the interest rate is typically way too low to keep up with inflation. You'd be just as well off having a CD—and *neither* are going to keep up with inflation."

"Got it," Pete said. "And the remaining 15 percent?"

"Ever heard of a 'fixed indexed annuity'?" I asked him.

Pete looked puzzled. "Aren't 'fixed' and 'indexed' kind of opposites?

"Not really," I told him. "An FIA's going to earn interest based on the *growth* of the stock market, but it's not directly *invested* in the market. It's linked to an index. These annuities are *principal--protected*—meaning you can't *lose* money, but they can also *grow* over time."

"Ah." Pete nodded again. "So out of all the annuities available, you only *love* about 15 percent?"

This time I laughed out loud. "Not even *close,*" I said.

"Huh?"

"It's more like *1 percent.*"

Pete looked at me quizzically.

"Explain, McFly."

I laughed again. "Most FIAs are going to have a fee . . ."

"And fees are bad," Pete chimed in.

"Bingo."

"That still leaves more than 1 percent, though," Pete said, doing the math in his head.

"Exactly, my friend. Of those *remaining* FIAs, you're going to have quite a few that will have a 'cap' on their growth rate. Usually somewhere in the 4–7 percent range."

"And caps are bad," Pete said.

I smiled. "Well, they're not *horrible*. In my opinion, 4–7 percent is still better than you'll do with most CDs. *Definitely* better than most savings accounts. But Pete," I said, "why should you cap your growth *at all* if you don't have to?"

"That's a rhetorical question, isn't it?"

"Now you're getting the picture, my friend," I told him, both of us now laughing.

I went on. "With the FIAs we use as part of your Retirement Trail Map—these 1 percent of all annuities, these best of the best, these personal pensions—you get *no fees, no losses*, and a percentage of the growth of the market with *no caps!*"

"Wow!" Pete said. "That sounds *great!*"

He grew serious. "Okay, Mark. What's the catch?"

I totally understood his concern. After all, we grow up being taught that if something *sounds* too good to be true, it probably is.

"There *is* a catch or two, Pete," I told him. "After all, insurance companies—like all companies—are in business to make money."

Pete nodded in agreement.

"The first catch—and I'm sure you caught this—is that you only get a *percentage* of the growth. One time-tested option allows you to earn half of the upside of the S&P 500 and suffer none of the losses: If the market goes up 10 percent, you'd have 5 percent growth. If it goes up 20 percent, you'd get 10 percent growth. But if the market *goes down*, you won't *lose* a dime."

"That sounds pretty awesome."

"It gets even *more* awesome, Pete," I continued. "These products also feature an annual 'reset,' meaning that each year the amount you made in the *previous* year is protected—just as if it were the principal. The annuity 'locks in' your gains. You can't lose money. You can't lose principal. You can't lose interest."

"I definitely like the sound of that," Pete said. "But you said there were *two* catches?"

I nodded. "The other catch is *time*. As with almost all insurance--based products, you're going to have to leave the money in there for a specified period of time."

"Ah-HA!"

I chuckled. "You can take out a portion of the money each year, usually from 5 to 10 percent, with what's called a PFW, or *penalty free withdrawal*. There'll be fees, though, if you need to take out more than that."

"How much time are we talking about?" Pete asked.

"It depends," I told him. "You can get these FIAs in terms of anywhere from five years all the way up to fifteen years. A lot of it will depend on your specific needs. We've found a 'sweet spot' is usually somewhere in the middle."

"And after the term expires?"

I smiled. "Then it's just like a savings account, but with a much better return. You can leave it all in there, or you can take out as much as you need with no fees or penalties. One hundred percent liquidity."

I could tell that Pete's interest was piqued, but I could also tell he had some reservations.

"This really *does* sound great, Mark, and I really appreciate you explaining it all to me," he said. "But I've been doing *so well* on the Nasdaq. Why would I want to put all my money into one of these FIAs, and get just a *percentage* of the growth, when—with my Nasdaq stock—I can get *all* of the growth, and have total liquidity to boot?"

"Ah, my friend," I replied. "I think you've misunderstood me."

"Huh? What part did I get wrong?"

"I never said you should put *all* your money into it."

"Oh." He thought for a moment. "I guess you didn't."

"That's the beauty of the Retirement Trail Map. Everything's geared toward *your specific retirement needs and goals.* There are no cookie-cutters involved."

"Cookie-cutters bad," Pete said.

We both laughed again.

"In my opinion cookie-cutters, when it comes to retirement plans, are *horrible*," I replied. "We'll figure out how much guaranteed income you're going to need. We'll calculate the size of the gap between that number and your expected streams of income (like Social Security). Then we'll create a personal pension to fill in that gap. Anything left over you can keep in the Nasdaq, if you'd like—although we may be able to offer you alternatives to that as well."

"Wow!" Pete exclaimed. "I'm *really* liking this!"

He paused a moment.

"But . . ."

"I know, Pete," I interjected. "You're wondering how you can be as sure as *I* am about FIAs."

Pete let out a sigh of relief. "It's not that I don't trust what you're saying. Our talks have been *extremely* informative. A lot of fun, too. But . . . well, you understand."

I *did* understand.

"Pete, have you ever heard of Roger Ibbotson?"

"Seems that name rings a bell. Some sort of financial genius or something, right?"

I nodded.

"Exactly. Ibbotson is a finance professor at Yale and chair of Zebra Capital Management. A few years ago, he wrote a white paper called, 'Fixed Indexed Annuities: Consider the Alternative.' In this paper, he and his team ran hypothetical return simulations from 1927 to 2016."

"Okay . . ."

I laughed. I didn't want Pete's eyes to glaze over with my financial nerd-speak, so I cut to the chase: "According to Ibbotson, '*Fixed indexed annuities beat bonds*.'"[35]

"Really?" Pete asked. "Always?"

I nodded again. "According to Ibbotson, always. He found that, over the period they studied, bonds lost money 13 percent of the time. FIAs *never* did."

---

35 Diana Britton, "Ibbotsen: Fixed Indexed Annuities Beat out Bonds," WealthManagement.com, March 7, 2018, https://www.wealthmanagement.com/insurance/ibbotson-fixed-indexed-annuities-beat-out-bonds.

"Well, *that's* pretty impressive."

"And it's not just Ibbotson," I said. "Nobel laureate Robert C. Merton,[36] Dr. David Babble,[37] Moshe Milevsky,[38] Tom Hegna,[39] Dr. Wade Pfau,[40] and numerous other top economists all say the same thing—that fixed indexed annuities are key to an amazing retirement. That's why they're such a critical component of our Retirement Trail Map."

"Really? They say that?" Pete chuckled.

"I'm paraphrasing, but yes."

* * *

And that, my friends, is how I explained the personal pension to my good friend Pete. And now to *you*.

Many leading economists (cited above) agree that the most efficient way of generating *guaranteed lifetime income* is found in the guarantees provided by an annuity.[41] I've had the pleasure of interviewing thousands of people about retirement planning. Most agree that they want a portion of their funds to a) be principal-protected (basically, safe) and b) still have the potential to

---

36   Robert C. Merton, "The Crisis in Retirement Planning," *Harvard Business Review* (July–August 2014): 3–10. https://robertcmerton.com/wp-content/uploads/2017/08/The-Crisis-in-Retirement-Planning-HBR-2014-Merton.pdf.

37   David F. Babbel, "Retire Smarter: New Strategies Towards a Comfortable Retirement," Comminsure, Commonwealth Bank of Australia, Sydney, Australia, October 2017.

38   Christine Benz and Jeffrey Ptak, "Moshe Milevsky: How to Lower Retirement Risk at a Turbulent Time," Morningstar, May 6, 2020, https://www.morningstar.com/portfolios/moshe-milevsky-how-lower-retirement-risk-turbulent-time.

39   Tom Hegna, *Don't Worry, Retire Happy! Seven Steps to Retirement Security* (Tross Press, 2014).

40   Kerry Petter, "'Safety First' Income Plans, Per Wade Pfau," *Retirement Income Journal*, October 10, 2019, https://retirementincomejournal.com/article/the-safety-first-retirement-plan-via-wade-pfau/.

41   See articles previously mentioned in this chapter.

grow. To be clear, any investment representative held to a fiduciary standard can offer investments (whether stocks, bonds, most annuities, or even real estate) that meet criterion B. But none of the investments I just listed satisfy criterion A at all. Those investments don't get you the benefits of growth without also risking your principal. FIAs do both.

Again, I'm not saying any old annuity will do that for you. You need the top shelf. The ones created to put power in your portfolio. With the best FIAs, you put up 100 percent of the capital, take on 0 percent of the risk (thank you, insurance companies!), and get to reap about half the rewards of an up market—without losing a dime from the inevitable downturns. It's just that simple.

A true "Best of the Best."

No losses. No fees. Uncapped upside. Liquidity. Flexibility. Patents. Topped off with a reasonable return.

I told you, though, that these FIAs are rare. That's why many Americans have never heard of them. In fact, the major brokerage shops may not have access to many of my absolute favorites. They're only offered by independent advisors.

I'm among them.

Again, this is a crucial component of the Retirement Trail Map. It's a strategy for creating an income *for life*. If done correctly, it allows your principal to stay intact, so that you're pretty much just spending the interest! It's a strategy to silence the enemy within, the one that keeps you awake at night wondering whether the market is going to boom or bust, worrying that you might have to "sell low" to salvage what's left of your nest egg during a market downturn.

Time and time again, I've seen retirees plan for glorious vacations with their kids and grandkids, only to have to scrap those plans when the market drops.

"We'll do it next year," they say.

And what happens next year? Sure, the market's rebounded, but now they need a hip replacement. So they put it off again.

Before you know it, years pass. Grandkids become teenagers, no longer all that keen on spending *any* time with their grandparents—much less an entire *vacation*.

Don't let this be you.

Be Like Shaq

As you know by now, I'm a fan of the NBA. I'm also a big fan of FIAs. That's why I was so thrilled to learn that Shaquille O'Neal now makes more money in retirement than he did during his NBA playing career.[42] As you can imagine, that was a *lot*. The four-time NBA champion credits this to some advice he got from his financial advisor many years ago—he began putting a million dollars per year into annuities.[43]

Obviously, we can't *all* do that. But we can do something similar: We can fund annuities that provide more income in retirement than we made while we were working. We *can* give ourselves a "raise to retire"!

---

42   Lawrence Castillo, "From the NBA to Annuities, From Free Throws to Guaranteed Income," *Gallup Sun,* September 24, 2021, https://gallupsun.com/index.php?option=com_content&view=article&id=15510.

43   Joey Held, "Shaquille O'Neal Reminds His Kids: 'We Ain't Rich, I'm Rich'. . .," Celebrity Net Worth, November 16, 2021, https://www.celebritynetworth.com/articles/sports-news/shaquille-oneal-reminds-his-kids-we-aint-rich-im-rich/.

What *specific* annuities did Shaq put his $1 million per year into? My educated guess is that Mr. O'Neal did the exact thing this chapter recommends: He got connected with patented, proprietary FIAs offered by independent fiduciaries for his own Shaq-sized retirement plan.

No, FIAs aren't for everyone. If your entire nest egg is $100,000, and you might need $30,000 in a year or two to fix the furnace or buy a new car, a FIA might not be for you; the surrender charges for early withdrawals can be prohibitive.

But it worked for Shaq. It worked for my friend Pete. And it worked for Joe and Deb.

It could've worked for Frank and Millie, too. Hypothetically, had they put their one million dollars into a fixed index annuity, they could have taken $50,000 every single year for the rest of their lives. They *still* could have followed the same diversified S&P 500 index. The only difference is that they would have gotten half the upside and none of the down. They would have suffered no losses and paid no fees. And that would have made more than $1 million difference for them. (At the time of this writing, they still would have had $1.2 million, rather than basically being broke for five years now.)

The personal pension isn't a retirement plan in and of itself. It's not a stand-alone solution. Rather, it can be a key piece to an overall retirement strategy designed to give you the peace of mind that comes with knowing that all your financial needs will be met, without any of the risks inherent in far too many other plans.

You can know that your golden years will truly be golden.

Chapter 9.

Retirement Pit Stop #2: Optimize the Opportunity, Minimize the Risk

Chinese military strategist Sun Tzu, in his fifth century BC treatise *The Art of War*, wrote that "invincibility lies in the defense."

He didn't say "success." He didn't say "victory."

He said "*invincibility.*"

That's what this chapter is all about.

We've talked about going on the *offense* in your retirement with strategies for maximizing your income. But—as any good coach will tell you—offense alone doesn't win championships. Retirement is the same way: Optimizing your investment opportunity without minimizing risk won't get you the prize.

I'm not going to talk about all the different ways to purchase investments. Endless books have been written on this subject. I do not subscribe to one type of investment methodology. We believe in creating a plan unique to each individual.

There is, however, one thing I've learned, one principle that has been proven to be universal in the financial world: **Investments are a matter of opinion.**

As Yogi Berra once said, "Predictions are difficult, especially when they are about the future." No one knows what's going to happen until it's already happened. Guaranteed income is a fact. Taxes are a matter of fact. Estate planning rules are facts. Even insurance—which may *seem* speculative—is based on actuarial *facts*. But investments? An argument can be made that they're *opinions*. They're speculation. They're guesses.

Let's build a Retirement Trail Map based upon facts and let the investment element be the one variable component upon which we rely the *least*. Let your investments be your "play money." Let it create your "play checks."

Back to the Mountain

American rock climber Alex Honnold is probably best known for his 2017 scaling of El Capitan, a 3,000-foot vertical rock formation in Yosemite National Park. He wasn't the *first* one to scale it, but he was the first one to scale it "free solo." That means he climbed that rock without any protective gear *at all*: no helmet, no rope, no harness, no ascenders or descenders, no carabiners.

Alex used none of the gear often relied upon by climbers to keep them alive until they get safely back on the ground.

He may as well have been climbing El Capitan *naked*. (He wasn't; as of this writing, that's still against the law in California.)

This kind of climbing is *incredibly* dangerous. I mean, mountain climbing itself is dangerous, but free solo climbing is the most dangerous of all.

You're probably saying, "That's *crazy*! Who in their right mind would *do* that?!"

Yet it's analogous to what many investors do as they scale their personal financial mountains. They have a "free solo" investing plan. They don't worry about the risk because slips in the market aren't fatal—after all, the market always comes back, right?

Well . . . *historically*, yes. So far. But even in the best of times, it's not a sure thing. More on that in a moment.

As I've mentioned, risk isn't necessarily a bad thing. It can be exhilarating. It can be quite profitable—*during the "grow, grow, grow" phase of your life.*

But as I've *also* mentioned, once you get in that retirement "red zone" (five years before or after your retirement), risk can be amplified.

Just ask Frank and Millie.

A Good Defense

Many of those who come to my office would say that free climbing is crazy. Yet that's exactly what they're doing with their money. It's a free climb until the markets freefall; then they panic and sell. They have no protection in place. No stop loss. No active management. No downside protections. Nothing. With today's technology, that seems nearly unfathomable to me.

Far too often, retirees who lose their footing end up stuck just "hanging in there." The sad fact is, most of them *have* the money they need to make it through retirement. Until they lose it.

They just need a better plan. A Retirement Trail Map.

As you've often heard: Use it, don't lose it!

Most of you have a life savings at your disposal. All you need to do is *protect* it, while leaving it readily available to you when you *need* it. Isn't that the whole point of saving anyway?

You need to find a way to guard your money against the devastating risks that could come your way. If your advisor doesn't have your money protected in some way, it's probably because—while he may be great at what he does—he's focused on the "grow, grow, grow" phase of life. You, my dear reader, have graduated beyond that to a different season of life. You may need a retirement guide.

As you've gathered by now, I'm a big fan of basketball. In fact, I still play as much as I can. So picture me playing defense . . . badly. Picture me just standing there, not making any defensive moves, not even staying with the player I've been assigned to defend.

If I did that, my coach would yank me out of the game immediately and say, "What are you doing, Mark?" Imagine if I told him, "Well, coach, I'm just playing some passive defense."

Something tells me I wouldn't be in the game much longer.

Your money needs to be protected with an *active* defense, not merely a passive defense. You don't have to know how to do this yourself. If you're unsure how to guard your money against market losses, consult a seasoned expert. A retirement guide will know how to guard your money against the potentially devastating effects of things like taxes, inflation, sequence of returns, risk, longevity, and market downturns.

A good retirement guide will help you *actively* manage the money you have invested. They won't just stand passively on the court and watch. At a minimum, your retirement guide will have a *tactical* approach. A seasoned, measured investment strategy and methodology . . . picture a coach with a gameplan to execute.

What you don't want (and I'm sure you're used to hearing it) is someone reciting the same tired words: "Just hang in there." "The market beats everything over time." "I was just about to call you to discuss that." You need a plan with a proactive approach!

As Sun Tzu said, invincibility lies in the defense. Get some defense.

Historically Deceptive

Let's go back to that "grow, grow, grow" phase. Most investment advisors place their clients' money into either mutual funds or ETFs (Exchange-Traded Funds).[44] There are a wide variety of fees involved, depending upon the type of investment. Very few have any downside protections.

"But Mark," you say. "Isn't the growth worth it?"

Not necessarily. A study from 2022 found that more than three-quarters of actively managed mutual funds underperformed

---

44 "Share of Households Owning Mutual Funds in the United States from 1980 to 2022," Statista, n.d., https://www.statista.com/statistics/246224/mutual-funds-owned-by-american-households/.

the S&P 500 and the Dow.[45] That's like buying a Corvette only to find out the dealer had dropped in a Pontiac Fiero engine.

Often disappointing, to say the least.

Of course, there's always *indexing*—that's what my friend Pete did with his Nasdaq investments. Index funds are designed to mirror the holdings and potential performance of a particular market. Even financial icon Warren Buffet says these are the way to go.[46] The fees are negligible (often just a fraction of a percent) and, again, the market always gains over time. (So far.)

But here's the caveat: People are *reactive.*

If you've ever owned a Chihuahua (or know anyone who has), you know what I'm talking about. They can be the sweetest little dogs, yet at the sound of the mail carrier or the ringing of the doorbell, they instantly transform into yapping killing machines.

Investors can be like those Chihuahuas. Especially in retirement. You may have been great at staying the course during your "grow, grow, grow" years, but—and I have seen this hundreds of times—once you retire, the market isn't simply "down 20 percent." As a retiree, you start to think, "I just lost three years of my retirement income. What am I going to do? I can't let this continue!"

The result? A *reactive* move to "get safer" at exactly the wrong time.

45 Josh Myers, "New Report Finds Almost 80% of Active Fund Managers Are Falling Behind the Major Indexes," CNBC, March 27, 2022, https://www.cnbc.com/2022/03/27/new-report-finds-almost-80percent-of-active-fund-managers-are-falling-behind.html.

46 Tanza Loudenback, "Warren Buffett Thinks Index Funds Are the Best Way for Everyday Investors to Grow Their Money — Here's How You Can Start," *Business Insider India,* December 17, 2019, https://www.businessinsider.in/personal-finance/news/warren-buffett-thinks-index-funds-are-the-best-way-for-everyday-investors-to-grow-their-money-heres-how-you-can-start/articleshow/72858534.cms.

DALBAR, a financial services market research firm, recently did a study that revealed the giant discrepancy between the market's returns and the returns that folks like you and me actually achieve. CNBC reported on the study's results: "Since 1988, the stock market's average return has been 10% per year. But stock fund investors have earned only 4.1% per year."[47]

Why? It's because average investors are *always getting in and out of the market*. And they're usually doing so at the *wrong time*. A drop in the Dow Jones or S&P average turns us into yapping killing machines, yanking our money out like a Chihuahua fiercely protecting its master. Unless you have nerves of steel like Warren Buffet or our friend Alex Honnold (who are *definitely* not Chihuahua types), you probably do the same.

How would *you* feel if the market averaged over 10 percent per year for the next thirty years, but over that same time you earned less than 4 percent? You would be devastated!

Don't let that happen to you. Don't be among the masses who suffer both the problems we just described: (A) holding funds or ETFs that underperform, and (B) suffering less performance because it is human nature to be reactive. Don't be reactive. A plan helps you to not react emotionally. So get a game plan and guard your money! Let a retirement guide show you options to still earn a very reasonable rate of return, but without so much risk. With less risk comes the ability to weather a downturn.

The best way to manage your investment dollars in retirement is to *optimize the opportunity and minimize the risk*. Sounds simple, huh? Yet the reality is that it's hard for most people to do. Shoot, it's hard for most advisors (stuck with outdated systems)

---

47   Ric Edelman, "You're making big financial mistakes – and it's your brain's fault," CNBC, August 1, 2019, https://www.cnbc.com/2019/07/31/youre-making-big-financial-mistakes-and-its-your-brains-fault.html.

to create that for you. That's why you should either use specific investments with tools to protect your principal (think harnesses and ropes for those non-Alex-Honnold-type mountain climbers) or create a tactical plan with a retirement guide—a plan that is custom tailored to your specific goals and trail map.

Why? Because your life is now about living the retirement you've always dreamed of. It's about earning money on your money, and letting that new money be your play checks. The fun stuff. The way you celebrate life and spoil grandkids. This season of life is not about an investment class. Optimize your opportunity and reduce your risk. Then go live the life you want.

I have interviewed over 1,000 retirees in my career. Many of them don't mind taking risk. Said differently: Not everyone is "risk averse." *However, nearly every retiree I have ever met is "LOSS AVERSE."* When we retire, we don't mind fluctuations—but we hate losses. Especially when they last. The right plan can help you maintain upside opportunity, while minimizing losses.

You don't need more money; you don't need an investment manager or a stockbroker. You need a better *plan*. A Retirement Trail Map will give you that plan.

Joe and Deb

When I explained all this to our friends Joe and Deb, they got it. They had actually done some amateur mountain climbing themselves and understood the analogy. Their friends owned a Chihuahua, so they understood *that* analogy, too.

They weren't really into basketball, but they still got the picture.

I stressed to Joe and Deb that the only risk they should ever incur after retirement is with money that's totally separate from what they'll *need to live*. In their case, we took $300,000 of their $500,000 nest egg and put it into a personal pension to create income for life. We attached riders for long-term care and inflation protection, so that they were guaranteed an income for the rest of their lives, with the safety harnesses that would keep them from falling off the mountain. The remainder—their play money, if you will—we invested in the market in a way that offered the potential for a great upside with only a limited downside.

Every retiree's situation is different. Every situation presents different options. What's best for Joe and Deb may not be best for *you*, and everything that I've presented in this chapter is meant to be construed not as financial "advice," but merely as education and information.

The most crucial element of the Retirement Trail Map is having the right guide. Someone who can help you navigate your way down your personal Everest—avoiding the pitfalls of taxes, inflation, sequence of returns, risk, longevity, and market downturns—to the retirement you've always dreamed of. Let's continue this guided tour on toward the next pit stop.

Chapter 10.

Retirement Pit Stop #3: Minimizing Taxes (Some Money Is Worth More Than Others)

Picture two houses of identical size and shape, both freshly painted and well maintained, sitting right next door to each other. They are both appraised at $500,000.

What if I told you one house was worth more than the other?

No doubt you would think that I had been out on this retirement hike way too long—that I'd finally lost my mind. Or maybe that I accidentally ate some "magic" mushrooms on my journey.

But here's some new information: One of the houses is owned free and clear. The other still has a mortgage of $200,000.

Now which is worth more?

Even though they are both appraised at $500,000 and therefore have the same "value," one of the homes has more utility, or usefulness. The owner of the first home can sell and net $500,000, while the owner of the second home, after paying off the $200,000 mortgage, will only net $300,000.

Although both homes have the same value, one is worth *way more* than the other.

The same principle can apply to your investments because different types of investments are *taxed* differently. That's the premise of our tax map.

A Tax Map

"Do you have a tax plan?"

Oftentimes, when I ask people this question, I get a blank stare. Kind of like the one you may have right now.

"Um . . . I plan to pay taxes. Is that what you mean?"

Not exactly.

Tax strategy is an integral component of the Retirement Trail Map. Why? Simple: because just as with investing, **it's not how much money you *make*, it's how much you *keep*.**

The IRS tax code is a map to help you find your way through taxes in retirement. But you need a guide. It's more than a little tricky to navigate. Picture murky swamp water. You need someone who not only understands how to *read* the map, but also knows how to find the "You Are Here" spot.

That's where we come in.

The Sky's the Limit—But Not in a Good Way

How would you answer the question, "Where do you think taxes are heading?" Do you think they're going down? Do you think they'll probably stay about the same? Or do you think they'll go *up*?

If you think taxes will go up, you're right. This isn't just what most economists say, it's what the *math* says. It's what *history* says. Sure, there are fluctuations. The experts don't say taxes are necessarily going to rise in the next year, or even the next five years— but they agree they *will* go up. This means that tax rates now are most likely as low as they're going to be for the foreseeable future.

Way back in 2009, the national debt was only $10 trillion. (It seems weird writing the word "only" before that dollar figure, but such is the way with national debt.) At that time, David Walker—the former US Comptroller General—wrote that taxes would have to *double* in 2011. Of course, they didn't, and our national debt has more than *tripled* since then. A quick visit to USDebtClock.org will show you that that's over $100,000 of debt for every single US citizen, or nearly $260,000 for each *taxpayer*. (By the time you read this, it'll no doubt be more.)

That's right: Every single taxpayer in the US would have to hand the government over $250,000 just to bring us to *even*. To get the government out of debt!

Isn't that a soothing thought? Doesn't that bring comfort to you? If it has the opposite effect and makes you upset—GOOD! It should! If your advisor isn't having conversations with you about how to be tax efficient, then you clearly may need a new advisor. If you're not taking the reins of tax planning on your own, then go find an independent retirement professional, held to a fiduciary standard, who can help you with tax and wealth strategies.

It's a *really big deal.*

Taxes are going *up.*

Not All Money Is Taxed the Same

I'm going to say something controversial. Something that may take a minute to understand. Then, I'm going to prove it:

Not all money is taxed the same. That means: **Some money is worth more than other money!**

According to the IRS, the average millionaire has seven sources of income.[48] Why seven? Because rich people have advisors who understand taxes. Those advisors understand what you are about to: the *source of income* matters most. This is especially true in retirement. You can maximize each source at the lowest level of taxability and create an astoundingly efficient tax plan. Please don't get bogged down in the minutia; you don't need to *understand* all the tax rules or ideas presented as a part of pit stop #3. I'm simply explaining the overall *concept.*

---

48 Jenny Bourne and Lisa Rosenmerkel, "Over the Top: How Tax Returns Show that the Very Rich Are Different from You and Me, IRS.gov., n.d., https://www.irs.gov/pub/irs-soi/14rpoverthetopbournerosenmerkel.pdf.

The bottom line is that you want to optimize your sources of income to pay the minimum amount of taxes on each.

The Six Most Common Sources of Income for Retirees

#1. Tax-Deferred: 401(k), IRA, 403(b), 457, etc.

This is the money that you put into your 401(k) or IRA (two common examples) *before* you pay taxes on it. It's taxed *when you take it out*, at whatever the ordinary income tax rate is at that time. This basically means that—whatever amount you have in one of these—you've really got 30–40 percent *less*. Uncle Sam's going to take a bite.

#2. Pensions

Nearly all American retirees used to get pensions from their employers. Now, hardly anyone gets them. However, if you are fortunate enough, you can create your own personal pension backed with guarantees that you will never run out of income. They are awesome! (See chapter 8.) This money is taxed the exact same as your IRA or 401(k). This is a key factor to appropriate Retirement Trail Map planning. Since IRAs share the same tax code, you should highly consider creating the personal pension with your IRA.

Income sources #1 and #2 are both taxed using "ordinary income" brackets. This is what we pay on our job earnings. It's ordinary. It is also the highest tax bracket we Americans can pay!

#3. Non-Qualified (NQ) Income

The easiest way to remember this is that this income *isn't* in a qualified retirement plan (hence, non-qualified). Dividends and long-term capital gains fall into this category. Under current tax law this is a favored tax rate. Some of you will pay ZERO on capital gains. Others will pay 15 percent (up to nearly $500,000 of gains) and then only 20 percent after that. Why is this favored? Because our government is giving us an incentive to invest our capital and make it grow. That is what makes our economy grow. We do what they want, they give us a bit of a break. Cool, huh?[49]

#4. Tax-Free Income

Everyone likes this one, but—as you might imagine—Uncle Sam does his best to limit income that he doesn't get a piece of. In fact, there are really just *two* sources of tax-free income: life insurance and Roth 401(k)s/Roth IRAs. Remember our twin houses example? These income sources are equivalent to the paid-off house. It's difficult to get tax-free money . . . but boy is it valuable in retirement planning! Even if it's just 10 percent of your nest egg.

#5. Social Security

Some people pay taxes on their Social Security; some don't. Weird, I know. Would you rather be in the "I don't pay that tax" camp? Thought so.

---

49   Pro tip: If you have a large capital gain from stock market investing or the sale of your business there are a multitude of tax breaks that can defer, reduce, and possibly eliminate the tax burden that devastates most business sales. Please reach out to your advisor (or my team) to find out more about how tax planning strategies may be able to help you.

The tax on Social Security depends upon the rest of your overall income plus half of your Social Security income. This is called your "provisional income." It can be very complex, but here's what you need to know: Some people will have 85 percent of their benefits taxed. Others will pay zero. Others will pay somewhere in between. It all depends upon the other sources of income. It can be immensely complex—I recommend you get help from a professional!

#6. Real Estate

Real estate is a highly favored income source for many retirees, in part due to its taxation benefits. You are allowed depreciation to offset against positive cash flow. If your advisor hasn't talked with you about the benefits of investing in off-market, wholesale, hard-asset real estate, then they probably don't understand the tax benefits. If you have over $1 million saved, you should certainly be looking into this. Another major benefit is the ability to "borrow" your equity by refinancing your properties. Borrowed money is not taxed at that time. This could be its own book. For now, make a mental note to speak with your advisor about the advantages and disadvantages of real estate investing.

Now that we have the basics of the six most common sources of income, how do we put it all together?

The Source of Money Matters Most

If you'll recall from my twin houses analogy, both houses had the same value, but each had a different utility or usefulness.

Now picture two retired couples. All four people are sixty--seven. They live in the same town. Both couples are making $90,000 per year in retirement. If I ask, "Which couple makes more money?" you'd think I've lost my way on this trail again, wouldn't you? And yet, because not all money is taxed the same, some income is worth more than others.

(Are you hearing this from any other advisors? If not, then you need a retirement guide!)

Remember our millionaires with seven sources of income? What's their strategy? In a nutshell: You take just the right amount of income from each of your income sources.

This is known as *tax stacking*.

Let's go back to our two couples.

Couple #1 is going to take $90,000 from their IRA, opting to delay taking their Social Security. IRA income is taxed at ordinary income rates. (Some would call that "standard tax rates.")

Couple #2 is going to take $10,000 from a Roth IRA (remember, that's tax free), $30,000 from their non-qualified brokerage account,[50] and $50,000 from Social Security. Go ahead and take a guess: Do you think couple #2 pays more, less, or the same amount in federal taxes as their neighbor?

If you guessed that Couple #2 pays *less*, you're right! While our first couple will pay under $8,000 in federal taxes, our second couple will pay ZERO (as of this writing—remember, the tax code is constantly evolving).

---

50   Assumes $15,000 of gains, $15,000 of basis. Funds from a brokerage account may be taxable to the extent that the withdrawal includes gains, which are taxable in many situations. This is not tax advice. Please confirm with your tax professional.

IRA: **$90,000** SS: Not started	ROTH: **$10,000** NQ: **$30,000** SS: **$50,000**
Federal Tax: **$7200**	Federal Tax: **$0.00** (Not a typo)

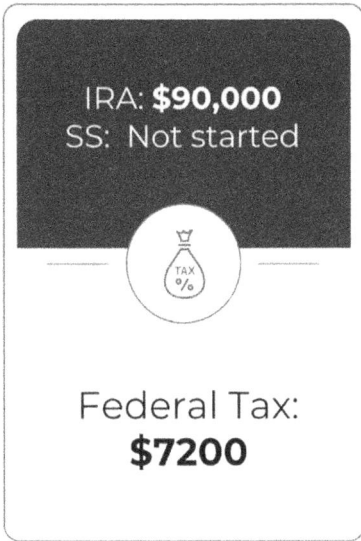

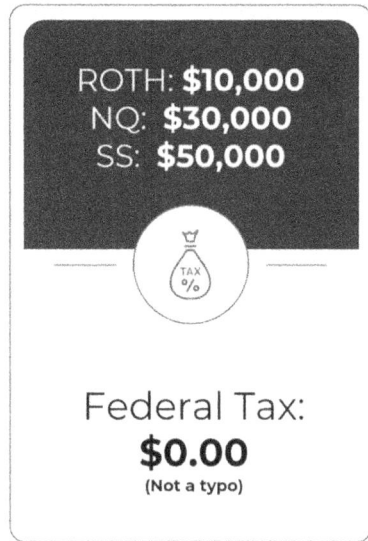

That's right. With this "tax stacking" strategy, you may be able to pay zero in federal taxation. Have you heard of this before? If not, a Retirement Trail Map might be right for you.

This isn't the only way to get to zero. There are many ways. The IRS provides the guidebook. We just help you navigate it.

Joe and Deb

Our friends Joe and Deb were like Couple #2 in the above example. By utilizing pit stop #3 on their Retirement Trail Map, we were able to create a highly efficient plan, keeping their income in a spot where Social Security remained non-taxed.

Their retirement was sailing smoothly along with all the income they needed, and we'd converted a portion of their IRA to a Roth. In 2008, Joe and Deb reached the age where they had to take the first RMD (Required Minimum Distribution) of what remained in their IRA. As I mentioned, those are fully taxable.

But Joe and Deb didn't *need* that money. They definitely didn't want to pay taxes on it. So what did they do?

Among those thousands of pages in the IRS tax code devoted to lowering your tax burden, there's a cool little item called a Qualified Charitable Distribution (QCD). So we were able to give that RMD directly to charity, fully tax-deductible. They also got to keep their standard deduction.

You've heard of double taxation? This is sort of like a double deduction. It's pretty awesome.

Voilà. No taxes.

If you like to help support your church, or have a favorite charity, QCDs can be a great tool. However, these are only for those age seventy and a half or over. Younger than that, and you'll need something called a "Donor Advised Fund." No, it's not a fund, nor an investment, necessarily. But it accomplishes the same goal as a QCD—it's just slightly less efficient.

The Retirement Trail Map will help you safely navigate your way from the peak of your personal Everest. It'll ensure that you make the pit stops necessary to get home with your retirement dreams intact. Minimizing taxes is one of these pit stops.

Judge Learned Hand—an immensely well-respected American jurist, lawyer, and judicial philosopher—famously wrote in 1934: "Anyone may so arrange his affairs that his taxes shall be as low as possible; he is not bound to choose that pattern which will best pay the Treasury; there is not even a patriotic duty to increase one's taxes."[51]

51 "Top 25 Quotes by Learned Hand," AZquotes, n.d., https://www.azquotes.com/author/6203-Learned_Hand.

Most Americans don't mind paying their fair share in taxes; they just don't want to pay *more* than that. I know *I* don't. I doubt that you do, either. If you don't want to pay MORE than your fair share of taxes, you have to see who might be making an illegitimate claim on your estate, and how to protect it. That's the topic of the next chapter.

Chapter 11.

Retirement Pit Stop #4: Legacy—Protecting Your Loved Ones from an Unknown Heir[52]

You may have seen the movie *Knives Out*. There is a scene where a millionaire's last will and testament is read by an attorney to all the kids and grandkids. The attorney says, "And the house goes to . . . And the publishing company goes to . . ." Each time—to the shock and dismay of all gathered—the benefactors are NOT any of those gathered on the solemn occasion, but rather someone new. A caretaker. Someone who wasn't a

---

52 None of this chapter should be deemed tax advice. Please consult your tax professional before taking any action.

blood relative. Without giving away any spoilers, the last will and testament left nearly the entire estate to someone unbeknownst to the family.

Chaos ensues. Lawsuits are threatened. The estate is thrown into turmoil.

Can you imagine a scene like this at the reading of *your* will? After a life well lived, after what you thought was proper estate planning, the very people you intended to take care of after your passing are instead left out in the cold. How do you think they would feel?

This happens every day. But it's rarely a love child that creates the chaos. Rather, it's that old, white-bearded guy wearing a star-spangled suit.

That's right, it's Uncle Sam, the unknown heir. And he sure ain't no love child. But he is certainly set to show up and wreak havoc at your estate settlement.

From all the studies I've conducted and books on taxation that I have read, I have come to the shocking conclusion that the average retired American (not just the rich) will leave more money to the government than they will to each of their own kids.[53] And the kids will be the last to know.

Can you imagine putting your children through such an ordeal?

My guess is that you don't want to. But if you don't pay close attention to this fourth and final pit stop, this is exactly what your loved ones will go through.

---

53   Much of this government "inheritance" will be paid in the form of federal and state taxes on their IRAs.

Pit Stop #4 on our Retirement Trail Map is all about legacy: giving you the peace of mind that comes with knowing that, when you're gone, Uncle Sam won't get a bigger piece of your estate "pie" than your loved ones do.

IRA Is an IOU to the IRS

In the last chapter, we talked about how some money is worth more than others. The money in your IRA is worth less than most. (I'm going to make an educated guess that a majority of your retirement savings is in an IRA, 401(k), or equivalent tax-deferred account.)

Let's consider another hypothetical example. Jay is a sixty-five--year-old average American. He drives a jeep, loves his wife Lisa, and enjoys life, even though it has been very challenging at times. Despite it all, Jay has managed to save $1 million in his IRA.

According to my projections, if Jay earns 6 percent over the next twenty years and takes all his RMDs, his nest egg will still be worth a whopping $1.8 million by the time he reaches his life expectancy of eighty-five.

Assume Jay and his wife Lisa pass away that year, both at age eighty-five. Their three kids will receive the money from Jay's IRA *after taxes at ordinary income rates.* That's the HIGHEST rate in our tax system. Jay and Lisa had their kids later in life. When Jay and Lisa are eighty-five, their kids will be in their late fifties or early sixties—still in their prime earning years. It is very reasonable to assume that the three kids will each inherit $600,000 taxed at a 40 percent ordinary income rate. (I may be lowballing the tax bill; many believe tax rates will be *higher* in twenty years.)

$1.8 million / 3 kids = $600,000 for each heir (before taxes)

$600,000 x 40 percent federal taxes = $240,000 in taxes due

That leaves each heir with $360,000. Not too bad—that is, until you dive a little deeper. Who's the *greatest* beneficiary of that IRA?

It's certainly not the children. It's good ol' Uncle Sam. His take of the $1.8 million IRA will be $720,000—exactly DOUBLE the amount that each child will ultimately receive. (Taxes of $240,000 per child, times three kids, equals $720,000. Uncle Sam is the largest beneficiary.)

Why will this disaster happen? Not because Jay and Lisa love Uncle Sam more than they love their kids. It will happen because they neglected the fourth pit stop. It will happen because creating an illegitimate heir has been the IRS's strategy all along.

No wonder we hate paying taxes!

Pit Stop #4 provides a plan to cut Uncle Sam out of the will with steps that can be taken while you're still around. Let's look at just a couple ways to do this.

The Roth Conversion

One way to keep Uncle Sam from becoming your biggest beneficiary is to convert that IRA to a Roth IRA. For example, say we plan to convert Jay's $1 million IRA to a Roth IRA over five years, $200,000 at a time.

Under the Trump Tax Cut and Jobs Act, this Roth Conversion falls mostly into the 24 percent tax bracket. That's $48,000 per year in extra taxes, or $240,000 for the entire amount.[54]

I know you're saying, "Yikes, Mark! That's a quarter of a million dollars!"

Yep. But it's also less than the tax burden would be if they *didn't* convert. And it's a tax burden that *they're* shouldering, instead of passing it along to their kids. Like life insurance payouts, Roth IRAs transfer to your heirs tax free.

This also benefits *the owner*. By eliminating the RMDs of an IRA, you can potentially grow your money quicker; you can focus on longer-term investments with greater growth potential, free from the constraints of the RMDs, which can often lead to "selling low." With this new focus, Jay and Lisa have the potential to earn 8 percent over the twenty years instead of 6 percent. How much do you think that Roth IRA would be worth when this couple reaches eighty-five?

$1 million? $2 million?

Nope. At the age of eighty-five, the math tells me this Roth IRA would more than likely be worth over *four million dollars*, 100 percent tax free.

Uncle Sam is cut out of the will.

Each child gets $1.33 million, tax free forever.

Uncle Sam gets zilch.

Did I tell you that I'm competitive and like to win? This feels like WINNING to me!

---

54 Everyone has a unique tax situation. This was the approximate amount our software calculated for Jay and Lisa. Please contact a qualified tax consultant for an accurate estimate for you.

This is what pit stop #4 on our Retirement Trail Map can do for you! But a Roth Conversion isn't the only way. And for many of you . . . it isn't even the best way.

The Family Endowment Plan

A Family Endowment Plan combines some of the benefits of a Roth Conversion with features of both long-term care and life insurance.

I've never been a fan of traditional long-term care insurance. The premiums are exorbitant: If you're sixty-five, they start at well over a thousand bucks per month—and that's if you're *healthy*. And they only get higher the older you get. Plus, if you're lucky enough to never *need* it, you don't have anything to show for all the money you've spent.

It's like "use it or lose it" on something you never want to use in the first place.

The fact is, though, that—according to government statistics—nearly seven in ten retirees will need some sort of long-term care.[55] Costs for nursing homes can range from $7,500 to $9,000 per *month*.[56] These costs can destroy legacies. They *have* destroyed legacies.

It's like having *another* illegitimate heir, this one depleting your estate while you're still *with us*.

---

55 Kate Dore "Most Retirees Will Need Long-Term Care. These Are the Best Ways to Pay for It," CNBC, August 27, 2021, https://www.cnbc.com/2021/08/26/most-retirees-will-need-long-term-care-these-are-ways-to-pay-for-it-.html.

56 Taylor Sansano, "Average Costs by State and Room Type," Consumer Affairs, November 10, 2022, https://www.consumeraffairs.com/health/nursing-home-costs.html.

I shared with you in chapter 9 that we attached long-term care riders to Joe and Deb's personal pension (their FIA).

Another option is the Family Endowment Plan. I also call this an *anti*-**long-term care plan**. This plan repositions some investments into an account which is 100 percent guaranteed and 100 percent tax free; it creates an immediate pool of funds that can be used for a stay in a nursing home or even home healthcare. This money can also be passed along to your heirs or left to charities. The investment can be *less* per year than what a retired couple would pay for traditional long-term care insurance.

Instead of "use it or lose it," it's "use it now or use it later." You can even cancel the plan and get back some (or maybe even *all*) of the premiums you've paid in.

For Jay and Lisa, this option of a Family Endowment Plan had an amazing effect. They kept their $1,000,000 IRA and decided to take 2.5 percent per year (only part of the interest they were earning) and fund a Family Endowment. That *one move* created an additional account worth an additional $1 million. They could leave this $1 million and the $1 million IRA to the kids. Or if they need to use this Family Endowment Plan for nursing care or home care, they have the option to do that. Dear readers, this is an excellent option that creates huge flexibility and, more importantly, leverages your assets to help you accomplish your goals. If this sounds interesting, please reach out to a qualified independent fiduciary who can shop around with all companies to find the very best possible fit for your situation.

A Family Endowment Plan isn't for everybody: You have to qualify (although the health qualifications aren't *overly* stringent). And remember, the Retirement Trail Map isn't a one-size-fits-all plan. It's tailored specifically to your situation and goals, and different strategies will work better for some than for others. A qualified, experienced retirement guide will show you how!

Retirement isn't a destination. It's a journey, and everybody's journey is different. Make these four pit stops along *your* unique path—each designed just for you, for *your* situation and goals. Also make the necessary course corrections along the way. You can find the freedom from anxiety and stress that defines the retirement you've always dreamed of. And you can leave a legacy that will continue after you're gone.

Chapter 12.

Happy Trails

Reading a travel brochure about the waterfalls on the Hawaiian Islands is one thing. Jumping from a cliff into the pool at the bottom of those same falls is something else entirely. Looking at pictures of sunset over the Grand Canyon is one thing, but it's an immensely different experience to feel the hard earth beneath your feet and breathe in the scent of dust and juniper at dusk as you get a glimpse of the Colorado River below.

One is easy. Passive. Simple. You can learn all about it without actually *doing* it.

The other, however, is called *living*.

In *Braveheart,* another of my favorite movies, Mel Gibson— as William Wallace—utters one of my all-time favorite quotes:

"All men die. Not all men truly *live*."

I challenge you to live your great adventure. Experience the retirement you've always dreamed of. Take the risks off the table so you don't have to worry. Hire a guide to get you where you want to go and show you all the amazing things along the way.

Jump off the cliff in Hawaii. Watch the sunset at the Grand Canyon. Take the European river cruise. Go. Do. Live! You worked your whole life for this! Let's go!

Implement what you have read here. Take action. You don't need more money; you need a better plan, with a better guide.

Thank you so much for allowing me to share with you all I've learned over the decades as I've helped couples like Joe and Deb—and individuals like Pete—navigate their way down the slopes of their personal Everests to arrive safely and securely at their dream retirements.

Retirement changes *everything*. Never have we ever traveled this path, and never have we ever faced such a hostile economic environment along the way. Yet with every change comes opportunity, and never have we ever been able to avail ourselves of many of the financial strategies I've shared with you in this book.

Bucking tradition is hard. For the most part, our entire industry has been hesitant to do so. They continue to push rotary--phone strategies in a cell phone world.

My mission has always been to tell the truth about retirement—to face the facts and adapt accordingly. That's why so much of what you've just read isn't something you hear from 99 percent of financial or retirement advisors, nor from the talking heads you hear on the radio or watch on YouTube.

The next move is yours to take. Retirement is a journey, not a destination. I wish you the happiest of trails along the way. May you avoid the pitfalls and enjoy the pit stops as you navigate your retirement journey.

Please visit our website at www.TroyerRetirement.com or email me at Retire@TroyerRetirement.com to find out how we can be your guides to the retirement you've always dreamed of!

About the Author

MARK TROYER has worked side-by-side with thousands of individuals and families over the past 25 years. Mark often says, "Retirement changes everything." As such, the traditional advice you learned with 40 years of savings, actually works against you in retirement. The result: devastating effects to the majority of hard-working American retirees. Mark founded Troyer Retirement to solve these dilemmas using simple plans that incorporate safety, growth, legacy planning, along with tax and fee reduction.

It is with this unique retirement planning approach that Mark has been engaged as a best-selling author, national speaker, radio host, published in Forbes, and a member of the Forbes Council on Finance.

Disclosures

Any names used in the examples in this book are illustrative only and do not represent actual clients.

Insurance products are offered through the insurance business Troyer Retirement. Troyer Retirement is also an Investment Advisory practice that offers products and services through Impact Partnership Wealth, LLC (IPW), a Registered Investment Adviser. IPW does not offer insurance products. The insurance products offered by Troyer Retirement are not subject to Investment Advisor requirements. Troyer Retirement and IPW are not affiliated companies.

The information presented is believed to be factual and up to date at publication; we do not guarantee its accuracy, and it should not be regarded as an analysis of the subjects discussed. All expressions of opinion are those of the author as of the date of publication and are subject to change. Content should not be construed as personalized investment advice, nor should it be interpreted as an offer to buy or sell any securities mentioned. A financial advisor should be consulted before implementing any of the strategies presented. The contents of this book are provided for informational purposes only and are not intended to serve as the basis for any financial decisions. Any tax, legal, or estate planning information is general in nature and should not be construed as legal or tax advice. Consult an attorney or tax professional regarding the applicability of this information to your unique situation. Converting an employer plan account to a Roth IRA is a taxable event. Increased taxable income from the Roth IRA conversion may have several consequences. Be sure to consult with a qualified tax advisor before making any decisions regarding your IRA.

Impact Partnership Wealth, LLC (IPW) provides services without regard to religious affiliation and the views of individual advisors are not necessarily the views of Impact Partnership Wealth, LLC (IPW).

Investing involves risk, including the potential loss of principal. No investment strategy can guarantee a profit or protect against loss in periods of declining values. Any references to protection benefits or guaranteed/lifetime income streams refer only to fixed insurance products, not securities or investment products. Insurance and annuity product guarantees are backed by the financial strength and claims-paying ability of the issuing insurance company. Troyer Retirement is not affiliated with the US government or any governmental agency.

www.ingramcontent.com/pod-product-compliance
Lightning Source LLC
Chambersburg PA
CBHW021938190326
41519CB00009B/1054